What People Are Saying about  and *Your Unique Purpose*

I wish I could get every person on planet Earth to read this book! That's not hyperbole. Let me tell you why. In this excellent manual for living a significant and effective life, Dr. Bill Greenman addresses head-on one of the greatest dilemmas of the human experience that every individual struggles with at some point: knowing that we are alive for a reason but not knowing how to discover what that reason is. Without definitively answering that vitally important question, how can we ever be completely confident and truly successful? What matters most in this life is that you fulfill *your* personal purpose and complete *your* divine destiny, regardless of what it might be. Learn the Master Principles and follow the simple yet profound plans that Dr. Greeman unpacks in this easy-to-follow book. If you do, *Your Unique Purpose* will change the world.

—*Dr. Douglas J. Wingate*
President and founder, Life Christian University
Tampa, Florida

Finding purpose in your pain and fortune in your follow-through, are mega-truths that come shining through in *Your Unique Purpose*. Dr. Greeman's transparency will transform you and his practicality will empower you. Please, do yourself and the world a favor—get this book, discover your purpose, and then tell others about it. I've read a lot of motivational books and attended many seminars and conferences over the past thirty-five years but this is an on-time right-now read!

—*Kimble Knight*
Chairman, Worship City Alliance, Nashville, Tennessee
www.worshipcityalliance.com
Director, Standing Stone Associates Program
www.standingstoneministry.org
Brentwood, Tennessee

You need this book! At a very crucial point in my life, I met Bill Greenman and he gave me pivotal tools to see and walk out my destiny in God. This book will answer questions, impart wisdom, give guidance, and inspire you to walk out your own purpose in God.

—*Brian Fenimore*
Founder and director, Plumbline Ministries
Author, *Exploring Spiritual Gifts*
Belton, Missouri

Our generation has a deep need for real tools to help us achieve the dreams and fulfill the desires within our hearts in order to make a lasting impact in the world. As those involved in the arts, entertainment, and media industry, we know of the importance of "working your plan" to reach your goals. If you want to find your purpose and design a strategy that will succeed, read this book by our dear family friend, Dr. Bill Greenman.

—*McKendree and Rachel Tucker*
Worship leaders, singer-songwriters
www.AugustYork.com

In *Your Unique Purpose*, Dr. Greenman helps bring out the primary driving force for a well-lived life: purpose. I have witnessed firsthand how lives have been reignited with new zest as people young and old have discovered their destinies using Dr. Greenman's principles, as laid out within this book. I believe this book will help you have maximum impact in this life. I pray that it will be the vehicle that awakens your transformation, as it has for so many others.

—*Bishop John M. Sikobe*
New Hope Church
Eldoret, Kenya

If you feel that your life is a circus of overwhelming circumstances and confusion, then you have missed discovering *Your Unique Purpose* and its Master Principles to help you to flourish and prosper. Dr. Greenman shares exactly how he has lived out these principles. You will be blessed to discover that your life has purpose. Living out that purpose is now your opportunity and destiny!

—*Dr. Cheryl Townsley*
Naturopath and wisdom coach
Colorado Springs, Colorado

Who among us has not repeatedly asked the question: "What is my purpose?" Bill Greenman gives us the road map, the simple steps necessary to discover and walk confidently in that purpose for our good and God's glory. What a blessing!

—*Mike Flynt*
Author, *The Senior* and *The Power-Based Life*
Franklin, Tennessee

Bill Greenman's brilliant book, *Your Unique Purpose,* is a must for every believer who desires to grow in fulfillment of destiny and purpose. As a professional life coach and motivational speaker, I am well aware of many seminars and workshops offered to the public, which cost thousands of dollars and cover much less information and insight than what you will find in this book. The Spirit-inspired revelations and keys found in these pages are truly transformational for all who will apply them.

—*Patricia King*
Founder, XP Ministries
www.Xpministries.com
Phoenix, Arizona

If it is your desire to live a purposeful, productive, and fulfilling life, then Dr. Bill Greenman's book is the "how to" that you need in order to achieve that life. This book will empower you to remove the imbroglio that has hindered you in the past by giving you the tools to discover, design, and direct your very destiny.

—Rev. Michael Kisabuli Masambu
Senior Pastor, Alleluia Sanctuary of Praise
National Director, Purpose International Ministries Kenya
Kamukuywa, Kenya

I have known Dr. Bill Greenman for over twenty-five years and have witnessed his compassionate, humble, bold, and consistent pursuit of, and development in, the many-layered spiritual art and science of helping people to discover their God-ordained purpose in life. He has forged sound and practical wisdom on this life-giving subject through his own faithful application of what the Holy Spirit has taught him in Scripture, as well as in the trials and blessings of his personal journey with our heavenly Father. He has refined the truths contained in this book within the rigors of doing business in the real world and the joys of building healthy inter-personal relationships. *Your Unique Purpose* is both a comprehensive overview and a field manual for discovering your destiny in life under our great and good God. It is theologically rich, balanced, aimed at the heart of matters, multifaceted, experienced-tested, relationally-aware, practical, and user-friendly. The Holy Spirit is all over this book and we will not fail to benefit by drinking from this well of wisdom and interacting with Him as we seek to live out what He reveals to us.

—Michael Sullivant
Author, *Prophetic Etiquette*

Dr. Bill Greenman simplifies many of the essential aspects of kingdom living. With his gift as a storyteller and by using his prophetic insight, he has blessed us with a readable and practical book on purpose to help us change our world.

—*Tom Deuschle*
Sr. Leader, Celebration Ministries International
Harare, Zimbabwe

Vain religion can cause Christians to listen to the words in the pulpit yet remain paralyzed in their pews. True intimacy with the Holy Spirit can cause people to awaken and see the kingdom advance through their spheres of influence. Dr. Greenman has done an excellent job writing a book that I believe is a must-read for those who are hungry to see the kingdom advance in their lifetimes!

—*Munday Martin*
Founder, Contagious Love International
www.contagiousloveintl.com
Antioch, Tennessee

Dreams…purpose…destiny—buzz words for the deepest longings of the human soul. In *Your Unique Purpose*, Dr. Bill Greenman gives practical principles if you are willing to work at finding your purpose, setting your course, achieving your destiny, and living your dream.

—*Bob Farrell*
Cofounder, Farrell & Farrell
Author, *When the Rain Falls*

YOUR UNIQUE PURPOSE

HOW **YOU** CAN
MAKE AN **IMPACT**
ON THE **WORLD**

DR. BILL
GREENMAN

W

WHITAKER
HOUSE

Your Unique Purpose:
How You Can Make an Impact on the World

www.purpose3.com
Bill@purpose3.com

ISBN: 978-1-62911-557-3
eBook ISBN: 978-1-62911-579-5
Printed in the United States of America
© 2015 by Dr. William Greenman

Whitaker House
1030 Hunt Valley Circle
New Kensington, PA 15068
www.whitakerhouse.com

Library of Congress Cataloging-in-Publication Data (Pending)

1 2 3 4 5 6 7 8 9 10 11 **U** 22 21 20 19 18 17 16 15

DEDICATION

This book is dedicated to every courageous man, woman, and child who has ever embraced a dream in his or her heart and set sail on a journey to make it a reality. Thank you for believing you could. Thank you for refusing to quit. Thank you for inspiring us all to greater accomplishments. We need your purpose, we need your destiny, we need you. Well done!

ACKNOWLEDGMENT

Every completed worthwhile journey is the product of many dedicated hearts and hands, such as the many wonderful folks who helped to produce this book. The following friends deserve special acknowledgment and thanks. They are the members of my "Master Mind" group, and together they helped me define this book.

Melanie Riekena, Kirk and Deby Dearman, and Mark and Brynn Gershmal, you are all such precious friends and wonderful comrades. Thank you so much for every ounce of encouragement, love, and direction you so selflessly shared with me.

Also, many thanks to my close friend of many years Dr. James Goll, for sharing the word of the Lord with me when I needed it most. Your are such a great partner and mentor!

And, most of all, I have to thank my beautiful bride, Meg. She is my consummately patient best friend and loving companion. I wouldn't want to do any of this without her, and I am so glad I didn't have to. I love you, babe!

CONTENTS

Master Principle #3: Live Your Destiny

FOREWORD

Are you searching for meaning in your life? Do you know why you were created? Are you fulfilling your God-given destiny and experiencing fulfillment as a result? One day, we each will stand before our creator God and hope to hear the golden words "Well, done! You were faithful with the gifts and talents I gave to you."

Are there keys to finding and fulfilling your purpose and destiny in life? How do you grow in your understanding and set realistic, attainable goals that still give you the capacity to dream?

Dr. Bill Greenman, in his book *Your Unique Purpose: How You Can Make an Impact on the World*, undoubtedly teaches us that there are keys that will unlock our purpose. In fact, Bill brilliantly and pragmatically gives us keys of the kingdom in this complete manual, which is a blueprint we each can follow!

For years, I have learned to pray the Scriptures. In fact, if you want to pray a perfect prayer, then pray the Word of the Bible. I have turned to Ephesians 1:18–19 many times as my guiding light.

I pray that the eyes of your heart may be enlightened, so that you will know what is the hope of His calling, what are the riches of the glory of His inheritance in the saints, and what is the surpassing greatness of His power toward us who believe.

The Lord would not give us a prayer in the Scriptures that is impossible to fulfill. Yes, you can know the hope of His calling! Yes, you can have the eyes of your heart enlightened and illuminated. Yes, you can stand with confidence that you have been found faithful before the Lord. In fact, finding and fulfilling your destiny and purpose in life is not a boring thing at all. It brings life! It brings joy! It brings satisfaction!

I have personally known Bill and his wonderful family for over twenty-five years. We have walked through the peaks and valleys of life together, prayed together, and stood together. I have seen my friend grow and change and yet always cling close to God and family, keeping godly, wise core values. With years of both marketplace and ministry experience, Bill embodies this message.

A coach of a successful athletic team has a game plan to win, not lose! A good CEO of a business searches out how to maximize the tools he has, how to strengthen the weak places, and accent the strengths. A quality senior pastor or leader of a ministry has God's vision in mind and works from that perspective.

As I certified life language instructor, I can assure you, this man knows the right principles, lives his own message, and that these principles work! This is not the next theoretical how-to manual. You really can find your purpose, plan your future, and live your destiny!

So go on an adventure. Dare to dream big! Seek the Lord and believe that He is directing your steps. Read and apply the teachings of one of my dearest covenant friends in life in this comprehensive guide. Read, pray, and apply the words of this book, and you will become a satisfied person who has fulfilled, is fulfilling, and will fulfill God's highest plan for your life!

With great joy,

—*Dr. James W. Goll*
International director of Encounters Network, Prayer Storm, and GET E-School
International best-selling author

PREFACE

When I entered ministry in the mid 1970s, I quickly became aware of a fairly universal need among Christians everywhere I traveled. I heard it echoed again and again for several years by the hundreds of people I taught, consulted, and counseled. Each person had a deeply felt need to find the reason he or she was alive on planet earth. Each asked, "Who am I?" "What's my purpose?" "How do I find it and how do I fulfill it?"

THREE BIG QUESTIONS

This prompted me to begin my own investigation as to just how widespread this heart cry was. Over the last several decades, I've asked people of all ages, races, both sexes, and most socio-economic levels on several continents the same three questions.

1. Can you explain to me your specific purpose in life—why you are on the earth—in one sentence?

2. Do you have a long-term written plan to assure you that you will live out that purpose?

3. Do you believe it's possible to live in the utmost confidence and productivity if you can't answer yes to questions 1 and 2?

I've heard the same unfortunate responses from virtually every large audience and individual. Consistantly, the results showed that less than 10 percent of the people I surveyed knew their purpose and less than 10 percent of those who did know it had any sort of a written plan to bring it to pass! That means that about 99 percent of the people on this planet are not living the confident and productive lives they could be living if they knew their purpose and had a written plan to help carry it out.

I feel fairly confident that you wouldn't be reading this book if you weren't serious about finding and fulfilling the destiny you were made for. I'm just as confident that you'll enjoy the journey in this book we're about to take together. It's the most important journey any human being can begin.

WHY THIS BOOK?

I wrote my first book on how to find your purpose in 1986, though I'd been teaching on it for several years. In 1996, the Lord instructed me to revise that message and get it to "all ages, using all media, on every continent." This was to be my part of "changing the expression of Christianity in the earth in a single generation." That's a commission many believers across the planet have heard—it's not unique to me—but it was a surprise. The Lord made it clear to me that when His people were confidently living in their divine purposes, unity would increase and everyone would see a difference. I agreed to do my best.

My first task was to rewrite my first book and give it a new title, *Discover Your Purpose, Design Your Destiny, Direct Your Achievement*. The book, published in 1998, is now being used as a textbook in a curriculum for second-year ministry students at one hundred satellite campuses of Life Christian University in twelve nations. Since then, I've written over a dozen more books, courses, workbooks, seminars, audios, and videos on the subject.

I'd like to say that God's first prompting was all the reason I needed to create those products, but that would be lie. The real reason is somewhat more supernatural and changed me forever. Let me explain.

While I was writing my second book in 1997, I became very discouraged. At that time, my son was deeply involved in the Dallas, Texas, drug scene, had been arrested a couple of times, and was facing possible adult prison—all before his fifteenth birthday. One day, I was feeling completely overwhelmed by his dark life and how it was affecting my wife, my two daughters, and me. I told the Lord that afternoon, "Why are you having *me* write this book? My family is in big trouble and I haven't been in full-time ministry for three years. No one knows me. I have no voice, no platform. I can't do this…. I quit!" God was not impressed, to say the least.

As I put my head down on my desk at that moment, something happened that I can only call a heavenly vision. I realize this may sound strange or even be outside of some people's belief of what God does today or what His Word says. All I can tell you is that it happened to me. I suddenly found myself standing in what I knew was the throne room of God for the judgment of Christians at the end-time. Jesus was on the throne, and a man I somehow knew was a Christian stood about ten feet before Him. Behind the man were thousands of Christians of all ages, races, and both sexes waiting their turn. Jesus leaned forward and asked the man firmly yet compassionately, "Why didn't you *do* what I created you to do?" The man was obviously very broken over the fact that he had *not* lived the life Jesus had ordained for him. He was weeping because he'd missed his life's purpose, a purpose the Lord had payed for with His own life. The man sobbed deeply as he said, "I wanted to…I just didn't know how to find out what it was."

Then the people behind this man, all as deeply hurt as he was, began to weep bitterly as they realized their own missed lives. They all began to cry out, "We didn't know how to find it, either!" I stood there dumbfounded with my heart aching for them all at the tragedy of their unfulfilled lives. Then Jesus turned to me, looked me directly in the eye, pointed His finger at me, and said in a very stern voice, "Why didn't *you* teach them?"

I instantly opened my eyes, jumped back in my chair, and gasped at what I'd just experienced. I was stunned that God was saying that if I didn't do *my* purpose by teaching others how to find and do His will for *them*, then I'd actually keep untold numbers of people from finding their purposes and fulfilling their destinies. I would miss *my* destiny by not helping them fulfill *theirs*. It shook me to the core of my being that day. It still does as I write this, and every time I think of it.

I can still see those people. I can still feel their anguish. I will *not* allow that vision to be fulfilled! So my commitment is to *give hope* and *build confidence* in the hearts of God's people, that they *do* have a unique and unequalled *value* in God's kingdom and therefore can have a significant, positive effect on the world around them. I'll do my part to inspire, educate, and activate believers in how to discover their God-given purpose and how to design the destiny required to achieve that purpose.

I *will* fulfill my purpose and live out my destiny with all the power I have and all that God will give me. This book you're holding is part of my destiny, my fufilled purpose. *You* are one more person I've had the opportunity to help hear, "Well done!" instead of "Why not?" That's why I do this. That's what motivates me every day. Now, I hope it motivates you!

SPECIAL INSTRUCTIONS

There are a couple of things I want to point out to you concerning this book before you start reading.

+ First, utilize only the strategies, forms, and actions in this book that *you* feel is needed to achieve *your* destiny. I'm not trying to bind you up with lots of activities. You don't have to employ every bit of information. Use what fits and leave the rest for a later time when it may be more appropriate, or never use it at all if you don't want to.

• Second, if you think this book is about a get-rich-quick formula or an easy path to success and prestige, go return it and get your money back right now! This is about *work*! You'll find no shortcuts to wealth, fame, or recognition here. But you will find easy-to-implement principles of life that will help make you successful in just about every area of your life if you apply them.

I do not think that I'm the only person responsible for helping every Christian on earth find and fulfill their God-given purpose. But I do believe I'm responsible for what I *can* do. We all are important. We all have a purpose. We all have a divine destiny to live. I believe that just about everyone wants to get started living out their purpose and destiny, yet most never do. Why? Because they don't have a map, a path to follow. I pray this book can be the beginning of that map, a path for you.

—*Bill Greenman*

INTRODUCTION

My theory, or the Master Principles Theory, is that there aren't thousands of things to do to be good or even great at anything (which includes fulfilling your personal purpose and destiny), just a few things. Only about half a dozen things or so are needed to achieve success in any area of life. I call these the "master principles." Find them, learn them, and apply them, and your life will change for the better, probably quickly. I'm going to share the main ones I've found over the last fifty-plus years with you in this book. The benefits of using these master principles are that...

+ Doors will open to you.

+ Relationships will improve.

+ Your mind and body will get healthier.

+ You will achieve more success faster.

+ Wealth will begin and grow in many areas.

It's not mystical or magical or even hard. It's not a secret, but it is special knowledge. Fulfilling your destiny is about taking these principles and unlocking what has you shut out from what you want.

Now, it takes real discipline to utilize the master principles, and plenty of it. When it comes to getting anything you really want, you won't get there instantly or without effort; but anyone can do it if he or she *decides* to do so. Hopefully that includes you. It took me awhile, but once I saw that I needed only to find and use a few principles to acquire anything I really wanted, I jumped in with both feet. I've searched for and found those principles for health, fitness, financial increase, influence, business success, relationships, marriage, ministry, and personal growth.

OPENING DOORS

I've been blessed by God to have accomplished many of my desires over the last sixty years. I've traveled the world, taught thousands of students, and written books and curriculums to help people live their dreams in their daily lives. I've surfed in the Atlantic and Pacific Oceans (what a blast!), earned a second-degree black belt in martial arts, spent seventeen years as a trapeze artist, owned my own circus for twelve years, been interviewed about my accomplishments more times than I can count, and spoken to crowds of ten thousand people and millions on TV. I married the woman I loved and have stayed with her for over forty years while we raised three awesome kids—now we're grand-parenting our four just-as-awesome grandkids. I have friends on five continents and many nations, and had successful international businesses and many successful failures (more on that in a moment).

None of that—I repeat, none of that—would have happened if I hadn't found and used the master principles needed to gain success in each area. None of that was by chance. And I still have a lot of items on my "life list" to accomplish before I leave the planet, if Jesus doesn't come back first. Those who personally know me will agree that I'm not bragging here—I'm just trying to share a reality of life that, if you can grasp, will make you unstoppable, an achievement machine!

Really, I'm nothing special. I didn't have an amazing family life as a kid, though it wasn't terrible, either—probably middle-class, average vanilla. My dad taught me only to avoid the back of his hand, though I did "catch" some great character items from him by watching the way he worked, accomplished things, and treated my mother. I never had a male role model who expressed care and concern and encouraged me until I was in college. I was an often drunk, insecure, young idiot who was headed for nowhere and getting there on time at the ripe old age of eighteen. But at that point in my short life, God turned me around, and I discovered how to live life with focused direction. I found the right principles and applied them vigorously, and they've never stopped working for me, no matter to what I applied them!

WHAT WILL YOU CHOOSE

But you know what else I've found? Very few people ever embrace these master principles. Why? They don't want the disciplines they require. They say, "It takes too long." "It's too hard." "I want to do the spectacular stuff *now*!"

I used to be one of those people, but I realized that few folks get to the top because few, including me at that time, are willing to do what it takes. They don't understand that the very things they shun *are* the very keys to everything they want! Incredible. Sad. Don't let that be you! I know that if I could change, anyone can!

When my life turned around freshman year at Florida State University in 1971, I began to get back to the master principles. Yes, I said "back." Slowly. I wasn't a rocket; I was a snail. But I was finally moving in the right direction. I had to go *back* to the beginning. You see, I had already been introduced to the master principles very early in my life—I just hadn't known it.

I'd like to ask you this question: Are you willing to embrace the discipline to do what it takes to get what you want? Just a question.

THE FIRST PRINCIPLES

I first learned the master principles at the YMCA as kid. My dad took me to the Y to learn how to swim when I was five years old (sadly, it's the only thing I remember ever doing together). It was there that I first heard about what most folks call "the fundamentals." I believe that the fundamentals are the foundation of the master principles, and take us to a higher realm of focus and learning. For me at the age of five, the fundamentals all were about swimming:

+ **Floating**

+ **Breathing** at the right time so you didn't inhale the water

+ **Moving** your arms and legs at the same time and in the same direction

+ **Diving** "along the water," not down to the bottom

+ **Obeying** the whistle

+ **Flipping** to turn

+ **Not drowning**

These are just a few simple instructions, a few master principles of survival and fun. How many principles could a five-year-old grasp, anyway? But I still needed a coach to teach them, explain them, and help me to establish them in my mind and body. (Remember that it's a master principle in itself, but I'm way ahead of myself on that, so back to the story.)

Those were the master principles of swimming. I went after them with a vengeance, not actually knowing that I was doing so, because it was just so much fun to me. I became the fish of the family, and I was good. I worked on those principles, or fundamentals. I began to compete in swim contests as I grew older and won a lot of them. In fact, I won too much.

I grew up in a town with few swimmers in my age group, so when I moved to a town that had a lot, it was not pretty. My very first meet, instead of the usual first place, I came in last place. I swam well; the other guys were just better. I was devastated. You see, I was never given the master principle to that situation—what to do when you are defeated, how to "fail successfully" when it doesn't go your way.

I don't remember a coach consoling me or encouraging me, though they may have. I walked away from competitive swimming at the age of twelve. I was "locked out" of what I loved because I didn't have the key to get back in. That key, or principle, was self-confidence. It's what helps us fail successfully, or, in my case, get back in the pool after a defeat.

If someone had just told me that I could have confidence in my proven ability, that I could grow and get better, I'd have done it. But I thought that, if I couldn't win every time, I shouldn't and wouldn't compete. I never went back to competitive swimming again. Sad. Ignorant. But I was only twelve, and I would bounce back playing other team and individual sports, even if only as average for the most part.

However, though I did learn the truth that the fundamentals could become the master principles of achieving my dreams, I simply concluded that swimming wasn't supposed to be one of those dreams. What about you—what's your story of failing successfully? If you don't have one, why not? If you have failed unsuccessfully, what happened, and how can you change the next time? We'll talk about this later in the book.

TEAMS

My next foray into sports was football. I wanted to play flag football…well, actually, I wanted to play it because it was the only football offered to my age group at the time. I tried out and made the team. To make the team, you had to do just a few things:

- **Run** hard.
- **Catch** a football.
- **Learn** a few plays.
- **Yell** loud.
- **Grab** the flag off the other team's guy with the ball.

Furthermore, I wanted to be the quarterback, so I had to learn a couple of more items, such as how to...

- **Hold on** to the ball when hiked to me.
- **Hand** the ball off to another guy.
- **Throw** the ball in the general direction of one of my teammates in the hopes he might actually turn his head and try to catch it (rare occurrence!).
- **Yell** loud enough so my entire team could hear the right signal on which to start the play, without ejecting my larynx onto the playing field.

So I did my best. I worked on those master principles, and I got better. I don't remember anything about any of that flag football season, but I do remember it was my introduction to team sports in a new way. I realized that, if we were going to win, my teammates and I had to do the basics and then turn them into the master principles. That proved to be true in everything I've done since. I haven't always stood on the platform of victory, but I have been on some great teams—in sports, business, and ministry.

THE POINT

What I'm trying to get across to you here is that the master principles are not that difficult to learn in any area you wish to excel, because there aren't a lot of them. Just a few. Whatever it is you want to do, you can probably do it if you simply take the time and make an effort to find the master principles and apply a few. The task is knowing *where* to find those principles.

So hereafter, I'll focus on the major master principles of life, which I've discovered and successfully applied in my own life. It'll be real-life stuff, not theory. It will cover a lot of areas, but there are not a lot of principles in any one of them. I hope that together we can unlock some areas of your life along the way. That would be a thrill for me. What are some areas of your life that need unlocked?

MASTER PRINCIPLE #1

FIND YOUR PURPOSE

"Love your neighbor as yourself."
—Matthew 22:39

This section is about finding out about *you*, your *self*, what makes you, you. The fact is that you are much more than you think. You are your personality. You are your experiences. You are your physical body. You are a product of your home, family, friends, and culture. You're a very unique person. Finding yourself entails delving into all of the above and more. While we can't go over all the master principles of finding you in this short book, I will give you some vital ones to help you get started. Check out my Web site in the "Resources" section at the back of this book for more materials.

1

WHY AM I HERE?

*"Man's search for meaning is
the primary motivation in his life."*
—Victor Frankl

THE QUESTION

What is *my* life supposed to accomplish? That's the second most important question you must answer (the first question being: Who is Jesus Christ of Nazareth?). Once you've dealt with Christ, you must discover exactly what you were created to do with Him for the furthering of His kingdom. As Christians, we hand the rights to our lives to the Lord God when we make Jesus the Master of our lives. From the moment we surrender to Him, our number one goal must be to find and to fulfill our God-ordained purpose. Of course, we as Christians can accomplish worthwhile goals by ourselves; but how worthwhile can they be if they never pertain to our ordained purpose, given to us by God Himself?

WHAT HAPPENED?

Let me share with you the events of two five-year periods of my life. The contrast is startling.

In the first five years, from 1971–1976, I showed little notable fruit…OK, no notable fruit. I attended Florida State University and managed to graduate with an A average after spending four of those five years climbing out of a C average. I joined that university's student circus (more on that later). I met Jesus, though you couldn't tell it by my actions during this time. I drank way too much beer, along with other unproductive actions I will not go into. Basically, I was average by every sense of the word. Well, maybe not every sense…there was the circus.

The next five years of my life, 1977–1982, were remarkably different. During that time, I spoke to thousands of people, wrote a book, worked as a professional trapeze artist and acrobatic performer traveling across North America, owned and directed my own circus, and trained ordinary people from all walks of life to be professional, quality performers. I was ordained as a minister; interviewed by radio and television stations, and newspapers; and helped other people get started in their callings. I acted much more like someone who *had* met Jesus, and was anything but average— all of which I assure you is not a boast in my personal abilities.

What made such a profound difference in my life in such a short period of time? What changed? Was it God favoring me? Did I get some big break? Was it fate? The simple answer is that I *discovered* the purpose that was only mine, and I made the *decision* to fulfill it! That decision led to the *knowledge* I needed to accomplish the *plans* of that purpose. It was hard work, and it was often lonely. But it was the most wonderful time of my life because I finally knew I was doing what I was created to do. I still know that! I want *you* to know it for yourself, as well! I want *you* to find *your* purpose.

"Every human being is created for a unique and pro-
foundly important personal purpose. Their destinies
matter. The task of life is to find that purpose and fulfill
it without apology or regret."
—*Bill Greenman*

SOME SERIOUS QUESTIONS

Were you born by chance? Were you born into your family
by a whim of nature? Your country, your race—is it all an accident? If you're a person who never knew your mother or father, or
if you were born to parents who were not married, or if you are the
offspring of a woman who was raped—does that make you less a
creation of God? Can anyone decide when and where and to whom
he or she wants to be born?

The answer to all these questions is no. No! You are *not* an
accident or a product of chance. You were supposed to be born in
your generation, and that's why God put you here. You are totally
unique! You were born for a unique and important destiny that no
one but you can achieve! Yes, life can be cruel, but with God, you
can overcome that cruelty and become what He created you to be.
And whatever that may be, it's meant to be wonderful!

*For this reason also, since the day we heard of it, we have not
ceased to pray for you and to ask that you may be filled with
the knowledge of His will in all spiritual wisdom and understanding, so that you will walk in a manner worthy of the
Lord, to please Him in all respects, bearing fruit in every good
work and increasing in the knowledge of God; strengthened
with all power, according to His glorious might, for the attaining of all steadfastness and patience; joyously giving thanks to*

the Father, who has qualified us to share in the inheritance of
the saints in Light.   (Colossians 1:9–12)

In his letter to the Colossians, the apostle Paul mentioned that he prayed continually for that group of believers. When I committed my life to the lordship of Christ, I made that prayer my own. I read it every day. I claimed its truth over my life, and I still do so today. I wanted the perfect will of the Father to be at work in me, and I desired to be filled with His wisdom and plan for my life.

Before long, the revelation of those words became a reality to me. I learned how to translate their truths into effective strategies for living. Soon they became a road to finding my life's purpose. It's changed me from a directionless person into an on-target follower of Christ. I want you to know that same change more than you can imagine!

These same principles will work for you. Why? Because they've been proven over and over again in the lives of countless others around the globe for generations. These aren't empty religious rituals. They are truths for all of us to understand. They demand work on our part, but we possess more than enough courage, energy, and desire to live them out if we really want to. *You* can do it! *You* can reap these same rewards! They are *yours* for the taking.

> "Great minds have purposes, others have wishes."
> —*Washington Irving*

WHY A PURPOSE?

In 2 Timothy chapter 4, Paul encourages Timothy to fulfill the ministry God has given him. Paul states that he has fulfilled his own ministry: *"I have fought the good fight, I have finished the course, I have kept the faith"* (2 Timothy 4:7). These are powerful words from a powerful man. If you're anything like me, and I am pretty sure you are, these words from Paul probably invoke a sense of envy. We all want to be able to say that we've run the race the Lord set before us. Unfortunately, most of us think that we have fought the fight, but our eyes have become so swollen from the beating that we couldn't find the course with a seeing eye, let alone keep the faith!

Paul's purpose demanded that he go to the nations as an apostolic teacher/preacher/mentor, not as the persecutor he started out as. Just like Paul, we can't let our zeal misdirect us. There will be people who will stand before the judgment seat of Christ thinking they've done a great job for the Lord, only to be told by Him, "I never knew you." You see, it's not about how much we do but about doing what He directs and ordains. It's about hearing the Lord say, "Well done, good and faithful servant, My son/daughter in whom I am well pleased!" That's what I want for you.

But let's get back to the question of why you need a purpose. The questions people most frequently asked me are, "Why am I here?"; "What's my purpose in life?"; and "How am I going to get it done?" Every person on this planet has a deeply felt need to know the answers to these questions, but few know where to start.

The New American Standard Bible states, *"Where there is no vision, the people are unrestrained"* (Proverbs 29:18). The word *"vision,"* according to *Strong's Concordance*, means "mental sight or a revealed word from God." The word *"unrestrained"* denotes "the absence of clear guidance or definite direction." A restraint, as referred to in this verse, is like a bit in the mouth of a horse. A restraint is there to direct, as it is used to guide an animal's immense power. In other words, if you don't already have a mental image, or a revelation, of God's personal purpose for your life, you'll find yourself lacking His guidance. You could be perishing in several ways.

+ Your mind may not know its possibilities.

+ Your body may not perform at its peak.
+ Your emotions may lack proper control.
+ Your relationships may be hindered.
+ Your finances may never reach their potential.

On the other hand, if you do have a vision for your life—a mental picture of who you are to be and how to get there—you will be restrained. You will be guided. You will have direction, and you will have the ability to reach your full potential.

> "More men fail through lack of purpose
> than through lack of talent."
> —*Billy Sunday*

MY OWN DISCOVERY

God doesn't want us to perish by lacking knowledge of His plan for our lives. First Corinthians chapter 12 states that God has a specific place for each of us and that He personally places us in it:

> *But now God has placed the members, each one of them, in the body, just as He desired.*   (1 Corinthians 12:18)

If you haven't discovered your God-ordained place, how can you be directed by Him? You may have visions, dreams, and goals you want to attain, and they may motivate you. They may even give you purpose and direction for a time. But only God's purpose for you as an individual will bring you the abundant, meaningful life He desires for you to experience. After five long years as a Christian with *me* in control of my life, I found out the truth of that statement—the hard way.

I discovered that no matter how much we may proclaim the reality of Jesus as our *Savior*, our lives are empty without Jesus as our *Lord*. Because I didn't have a revealed word from God, I didn't have God's guidance fully active in my life. Instead, I had my own dreams, and so I was perishing to an extent. There was a void in my life. Finally in 1976, I cried out to God, "Okay, Father, no longer my will, but Your will be done in my life!" It was then that both my spiritual and natural life ignited.

Almost immediately, God planted His vision of a Christ-centered circus in my heart, which we began in 1978. That vision showed me the major part of my purpose was to be a minister, which fulfilled me in a way no other dream had done before. I was totally directed by that circus vision. I was restrained, directed, and guided because of it. My total motivation stemmed from that vision because it was part of God's purpose and plan for my life. (You can see more about our Circus Allelia years on our Web site www.purpose3.com.)

And when Circus Alleluia Ministries was laid to rest in 1989, I was given the next phase of my purpose and destiny. This phase, though of a different expression, was completely in line with ministering the gospel of Christ and helping others to do the same. My motivation was not diminished; it was merely redirected, just as you turn a horse by pulling on the reins.

I've always had a sense of destiny in my heart. Since I was a kid, I wanted to be a professional entertainer of some sort. But I found out that my real destiny was helping others discover their own life callings. Fortunately, I got to take my performing dream with me, and it turned out to be much more rewarding than using it all just for myself.

God has a purpose for your life. He wants you to know it. That purpose, or vision, may be unusual, like the circus. But if it's God's will for you, I guarantee you that, by living it out with Him, you will receive no greater feeling of security in the entire world.

Ultimate success is placing all that you are into God's hands, so that He can do with it as He pleases, and then working with Him to fulfill His will for you. The day I made that decision was the day my life took off like a rocket! I believe that yours will too. Find your purpose. Find direction. Find the destiny ordained for you! It's waiting for you right now. I'll help you discover it through the tools in this book.

YOUR PLACE IN THE SON

In later chapters, we'll discuss exactly how to discover and live out your personal purpose and destiny; right now, let's talk about the general vision the Lord has for you and every Christian. The Father has set certain things (from which none of us is exempt) before His church to accomplish. These universal orders will not only cause the master plan of God to be realized by His body but will also assist in the preparation of the individual believer to live out his or her purpose.

In John 15:16 and Matthew 5:14–16, Jesus makes the following bold and far-reaching proclamations to His followers:

> *You did not choose Me but I chose you, and appointed you that you would go and bear fruit, and that your fruit should remain.* (John 15:16)

> *You are the light of the world. A city set on a hill cannot be hidden; nor does anyone light a lamp and put it under a basket, but on the lampstand, and it gives light to all who are in the house. Let your light shine before men in such a way that they **may see your good works, and glorify your Father who is in heaven.*** (Matthew 5:14–16)

What a mandate! What a powerful commission! By making these statements, Jesus is equating His church, in its ability to bring God into a world that doesn't know Him, with Himself. He is clearly saying, "I've been the Light. You be that light now. Go and do what I did. Be a giver. Be a healer. Be a vessel for the power of God to flow through to meet the needs of people. Let your good deeds reflect the glory of God! Don't be afraid, and don't hide what I'm giving you. Men in a dark place are drawn to the light. Be that light for them."

"Purpose is the engine,
the power that drives and directs our lives."
—John R. Noe

FINAL THOUGHTS

As exciting as Christ's command is, much lies behind its simple message. Being the light of the world requires more than a directive from the lips of Jesus. If we fail to put wings to His words, they will never become a reality in our lives. Notice the small but pivotal set of letters that spell the word "*let*" in Matthew 5:16. With that one word, Jesus unquestionably places the responsibility for doing His words on the all-too-human shoulders of His church. That choice is unequivocally ours.

I realize that there are many questions about how and where and with whom we live out the purpose of our life. I'll do my best to give you practical answers, things you can do today, in the next few chapters. But first I want you to understand the magnitude of who you are and just how far-reaching your life can be. I believe that each of our destinies is meant to change the world in some way. And, actually, there are only seven major areas in society in which we can get that done.

2

THE SEVEN MOUNTAINS

"Let your light shine before men in such
a way that they may see your good works,
and glorify your Father who is in heaven."
—Matthew 5:16

THE DOUBLE COMMISSION

In the 1970s, Dr. Bill Bright, founder of Campus Crusade for Christ, and Loren Cunningham, founder of Youth With A Mission, each had a very profound encounter with God. In those encounters, the Lord told them to share what He showed them with each other. When they got together, they discovered they had been given the exact same information! The Lord had told them about seven mountains that represented the seven areas of influence in any given society. Then an eighth mountain appeared, looming high above and the other seven. This mountain represented the kingdom of heaven—the ultimate mountain of influence. The Lord also spoke to them about the "mind molders."

WHO ARE THE MIND MOLDERS?

The mind molders are a very small percentage of any population—good or bad—that heavily influences its society through positions of leadership and communication. This gives the mind molders the ability to direct the population's course of thoughts and therefore actions. The mind molders are the people with authority to present their agendas in the seven mountains of influence listed below. Some people think there is a global conspiracy at work between the mind molders that has them all purposefully working together to shape nations one way or another. Others don't think such a conspiracy exists. Regardless of who is right, mind molders exist in all societies and effectively present their particular views. Let's take a look at the seven mountains of societal influence, and then we'll discuss your part in them.

THE SEVEN MOUNTAINS (REALMS) OF SOCIETAL INFLUENCE

1. *Family:* The family unit is the very foundation of God's kingdom and every race and nation on earth. This is meant to be and usually is the most influential of all the mountains.

2. *The True Church:* This refers to gatherings of believers today that live closely like the early church in the book of Acts, with total commitment to Christ, to His Word, and to His kingdom. This type of church is built on families unified by the Spirit of God. These Christians understand and walk in the ways of God's covenant of blessing and commitment to share His love and truth with all mankind.

3. *Government:* God created covenants with families and nations, most prominently the Jews and the Christians. Governments are created by people as a means to protect and bless them, but are only as good as those who run

it. (Read Kings, Chronicles, and Judges for examples of good and bad governmental leadership.)

4. *Education:* There are over two hundred references to wisdom, knowledge, and understanding in Proverbs alone. Education is needed to increase the value of individuals and thereby strengthen a nation so that it keeps up with the progress of the world and may even lead that progress.

5. *Commerce:* God's plan for business and finances is found in 2 Corinthians 9:8, which states that God's will for His people is an abundance for every good deed. Commerce is to create prosperity for anyone willing to work. It brings new innovations, technology, health, and blessing, with the end point being blessing others, not simply self.

6. *Entertainment:* This includes sports, movies, TV, theater, music, and so forth. Entertainment is merely helping people take their minds off one thing and put them on another. It's meant to bring emotional and physical pleasure, joy, excitement, and oftentimes deep emotions and thought. It should promote and exemplify moral strength to help people live morally strong.

7. *Media:* This refers to the many tools of communication, such as film, TV, radio, the Internet, books, and magazines. Again, it should strengthen all other mountains and therefore the people. It must work hard to be as unbiased and morally upright as possible to properly help people be strong and moral. This is one of the most powerful of all the mountains due to its ability to so quickly and consistently reach so many people.

These seven mountains of influence teach us, inspire us, compel us, force us, and distract us in specific ways and directions.

They don't necessarily tell us how to think, but they give us the choices to think about. Darkness prevails in the absence of light. However, light can't be stopped by darkness, no matter how thick that darkness may be. And we, believing Christians, are the light of the world! Therefore, in order to assure that darkness does not control the seven mountains of influence, we must find our place in those mountains and let our light shine brightly.

A STRATEGY

If we ever believe ungodly mind molders are in control of any aspect of our societies, we must then engage them as fellow mind molders who believe and act as Jesus did. Our focus should not be to simply dump them out and take their place. On the contrary, our objective is that which Christ gave before He ascended—to go and preach, teach, and make disciples. That's not dominion by force—it's not about domination at all—it's about relationship. We are to love those we disagree with. It's the job of the Holy Spirit to convict them of any sin. We simply let His light shine through us in word and in deed—the rest is up to Him.

By discovering our specific purpose, we can then see which of the seven mountains our purpose fits into. Then we live our destiny with the understanding that we are to affect those mountains with God's life flowing through us, by loving people no matter what they are like. It doesn't mean we are to be doormats or spineless—we don't compromise what we believe, and we should be well educated and able to share what we believe without being obnoxious. We simply live as Christ did and trust God with the rest. If we do, we will see miracles in the lives of the people in our mountains of influence and possibly even in the lives of the mind molders. When this happens, God can change our nations. We may even become mind molders of the seven mountains ourselves. But that's up to God.

This strategy will require several things to take place.

1. *A change of thinking* about how Christians are to live "in the world but not of the world." (See John 17:16.) We are from the realm of heaven, and that realm envelops and influences the other seven lesser realms. All God needs to accomplish this is willing people He can work through.

2. *Christians discovering, designing, and living out* the specific purpose God intended for them in all the mountains they live in, not just the church realm. It's not about filling church buildings on Sunday morning; it's about changing the other six realms.

3. This will release the favor and power of God through us to *mold the minds of those around us.* When someone else sees the miraculous, loving power of God released through a person living out their God-given purpose, he or she is either drawn to it or repulsed by it, as Jesus displayed for us. Most people were and still are drawn to Him.

4. *We must seek quality relationships* with people in present positions of authority in the seven realms, so that we can tap into the power of God to help those people lead correctly (such as Joseph, Daniel, Esther, and Nehemiah did). The favor of God will give us those relationships, and the opportunity to turn their minds toward His realm, but only if we are adequately prepared with a message worth listening to instead of just zealous talk. Such favor will also allow those of us called to become mind molders to step into those roles more easily.

KNOWING YOUR PURPOSE MATTERS

Being zealous is not enough, especially in these last days of human history. To obey is better than to sacrifice, and zeal is not necessarily obedience. We must find our specific purpose and the commissions that go with it. Then we must do them. It's only when we are ready to do them without ambition and self-exaltation as our motives that the Lord can fully release us. That is often a decade or more process. When we discover our specific purposes and then the specific societal mountains we are to take part in, we have to trust God to supply the favor and resources to have the affect He desires. That's our reason for being here.

As we discover more of our purpose and the unique destiny it demands, it will be obvious which of the societal mountains we are to live out to fulfill that purpose. This will give us opportunities to affect those around us in those mountains with the gospel of Christ. Make no mistake about it—you *will* affect in some way one or more of the seven societal mountains of influence, and therefore your purpose will create change in this world.

We can't be afraid to counsel the pharaohs and kings of our day, as did Joseph, Esther, and Daniel, for our influence may save entire nations. And we can't think our specific purpose or place is insignificant in any mountain we may be a part. It takes us all being who we were made to be to change the world for the better and for our Lord.

VALUE VS. VALUE

There are different levels of authority and responsibility in all the societal mountains I've listed above. Your position and economic state in any or several will correspond to the value you bring to that realm. For instance, a medical doctor will have an entirely different value in the marketplace than a carpenter. Why? Because of the value of his knowledge and expertise. Doctors save lives; carpenters build things. Their values in society are quite different. The wonderful thing is that we can change our value—our level of influence and income—in society through education and developing our skills.

Now contrast that marketplace or societal value with the value of every human being in the eyes of God. Here we *all* are equal. This is the value of our soul. Christ died for that value—no matter who we are or what our societal or marketplace value may be. This value is completely determined by God alone and cannot be changed. We all are of equal value to the Lord.

But because man as a whole has not understood this contrast of values there has been slavery, genocide, war, and jealousy. When we look only at the societal value of a person we operate only in the seven mountains of man and not in the mountain of God. But we are called to do both. We must understand our value to society and the mountains in which we will live, and at the same time be content that we are of the same value to God regardless of our value to society. You must believe this. And it will give you peace that just because another believer or an unbeliever goes to a higher level in a societal mountain, you have the same value as they do to God.

TIMING IS EVERYTHING

Abraham, Joseph, David, Esther, and Paul all had extraordinary purposes and destinies. They were the most powerful mind molders of their day, perhaps ever, but each had to wait decades until God said, "Now go!"

When their time came, others recognized it and came alongside to help them become known and accomplish their calls. Abraham had his servants. Joseph had Pharaoh. David had his mighty men. Esther had Mordecai. Paul had Barnabas. Jesus had His twelve diciples. You and I are no exception; only the timing and the names of our helpers will differ for each of us.

That doesn't mean we can't or won't achieve great things for ourselves, others, and the kingdom of God during what I call "the patience years." It simply means that our greatest achievements will not come, our greatest ability to effect the mind molders and therefore the seven mountains of a nation, will not occur until *we* have been molded ourselves; until we have been transformed into that specific person whom God can use to change the world, to shape human history in some small or large way.

As Abraham Lincoln—a man who had many more political defeats than victories, more heartache than love—said, "I will study, I will prepare, and then my time will come." It did come. In a few short years, Lincoln changed America and, through it, the world. And it will come for you and me. That must be our attitude and motto as we look to fulfill our purpose on this earth, in this time, in this nation or others. We matter. Our purpose matters. Our destiny matters.

FINAL THOUGHTS

As I said, mind molders control the seven mountains of influence and so control the nations. How those people influence should be influenced by Christians, or they should be Christians themselves, because our mountain—the kingdom of God—supersedes all other mountains. It's not about domination but about genuine, caring relationships with those mind molders and all who we touch, because God is deeply in love with them. The favor of God overwhelms natural and/or demonic favor. The love of God outshines the shadows of hate and fear. The blessing of God conquers the curses of sin. We can lose only by doing nothing—as history has proven. Let those days not be duplicated in our lifetime. We must be who we were made to be, and we must be sure we get His divine order flowing in our lives. We have to put first things first.

3

FIRST THINGS FIRST

"Whatever we value most,
we will rarely be willing to compromise."
—*Bill Greenman*

VALUES

In the last chapter, I spoke about a contrast of human values. Now let's talk about what you value. It comes down to what you value most. If God is not the most important figure in your life, you won't be able to fulfill your purpose, because He will *always* be in the center of any purpose He gives. He asks us to take care of people, thereby bringing glory to Him. But if we don't value people, we can't glorify Him, because helping people is how its done.

"Our value is the sum of our values."
—*Joe Batten*

You will always do what you value most. In the long term, you can't sustain a false love of people or a fake desire to point others to the goodness of God. You either mean it or you don't, and the truth always prevails. That's a fact.

There was a time when the church chose to rebel against this order. That decision plunged the world into one of the worst times in its existence; history calls it the Dark Ages. During that time, the Word of God was almost lost. The candle of God's church flickered as though it might go out forever. But the Lord always chooses and appoints people to bear His light, and these children of God slowly emerged to spread the good news of His love.

Perhaps you're in a "dark age," or haven't yet discovered how to let your light shine. Maybe you still struggle with what you value most. Let me ask you some questions that may help reveal conflicts between you and God. Do you put people after things? Is God Someone to be feared but not known? What do you value most in this life?

GOD'S UNIVERSAL COMMISSION FOR HIS CHILDREN

Our task is lining up with God's values and then finding out how to live by them. If you have yet to discover the basics of how to live in God's value system, below are some simple steps you can take. They are the universal commission God has for all His children.

COMMISSION #1: MAINTAIN LORDSHIP

In Matthew 6:33, we find the famous passage: *"But seek first His kingdom and His righteousness, and all these things will be added to you."* The Greek word for *"seek"* in this verse is taken from the Hebrew word for *worship*. In fact, upon studying both the Old and New Testaments, I discovered five different words that have been translated into the English word *seek*. For all but one of those words, either the primary or secondary meaning is defined as worship or prayer; and for all, the root meaning is that of searching for something.

To seek, then, means to search for something through prayer and worship. We don't need to read tons of books or make great pilgrimages in search of God or His kingdom. We need only to lift our voices and bend our knees in worship and prayer. The Bible is quite clear on this subject, as can be seen in the following verses:

> Then Jesus said to him, "Go, Satan! For it is written, 'YOU SHALL WORSHIP THE LORD YOUR GOD, AND SERVE HIM ONLY.'" (Matthew 4:10)

> Therefore I urge you, brethren, by the mercies of God, to present your bodies a living and holy sacrifice, acceptable to God, which is your spiritual service of worship. And do not be conformed to this world, but be transformed by the renewing of your mind, so that you may prove what the will of God is, that which is good and acceptable and perfect. (Romans 12:1–2)

Worship is the first aspect of maintaining lordship. These verses state that not only are we to worship God only, but that Jesus is the recipient of our praises. Even our physical bodies are to be a form of worship. Check yourself right now on that one. Our Father leaves no room for speculation. He orders us to worship, then He explains to whom our worship is given. Finally, He informs us that our very lives are to worship the Lord.

The study of God's Word is the second aspect of maintaining lordship.

> But He answered and said, "It is written, 'MAN SHALL NOT LIVE ON BREAD ALONE, BUT ON EVERY WORD THAT PROCEEDS OUT OF THE MOUTH OF GOD.'" (Matthew 4:4)

In this verse, Jesus states that God's Word is actually more important than food for our bodies. Not that we should neglect the care and feeding of our physical bodies, but we should realize that our spirits need the Word of God even more than our bodies need food. Why? Food only energizes our bodies, but the Word touches our entire being:

> *All Scripture is inspired by God and profitable for teaching, for reproof, for correction, for training in righteousness; so that the man of God may be adequate, equipped for every good work.* (2 Timothy 3:16–17)

The Word of God is a multifaceted instrument with which the Father can mold and shape us into the people we were meant to be. It can correct a fault, instruct in service, convict, or reprove. God's life-changing Word has the supernatural ability to turn rebels into godly men and women. But as with anything in God's kingdom, we have the final say in how much, if at all, His Word affects us. We must make a quality effort to study and understand the Scriptures. The Holy Spirit is our teacher, and He will take what we're studying and reveal its full meaning to us.

> *Flesh and blood did not reveal this to you, but My Father who is in heaven. I also say to you that you are Peter, and upon this rock I will build My church; and the gates of Hades will not overpower it.* (Matthew 16:17–18)

This is known as revelation knowledge, and Jesus said it was the rock upon which He would build His church. However, the Holy Spirit can reveal only the Word we get down inside us. For that very reason, it's our duty to establish a solid and personal relationship with God.

> *Why do you call Me, "Lord, Lord," and do not do what I say?* (Luke 6:46)

> *But prove yourselves doers of the word, and not merely hearers who delude themselves.* (James 1:22)

See Figure #1 below.

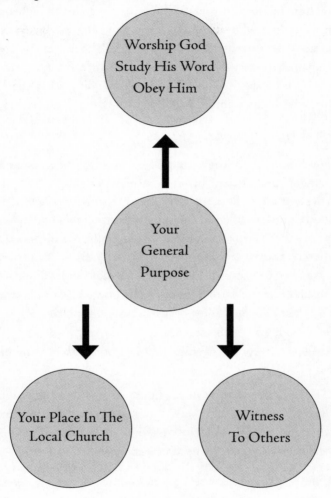

The final aspect of maintaining the lordship of Christ in our lives is obedience. Jesus did not mince words on this subject, as we can see by the above verses.

Doing whatever the Holy Spirit reveals to you from the Word of God is mandatory if you're to serve Him fully. (We'll discuss how to confirm that you're hearing God's voice in your personal prayer time in later chapters.) Many people claim to be believers, but it's the doer who will stand strong and immovable when the floodwaters of life crash upon him or her. The storms of life will come against us regardless of how prepared we are. Digging deep into the solid rock of God's Word means doing what the Word instructs, and it guarantees you'll make it through any storm.

COMMISSION #2: LIVING LOCALLY

Functioning in a local group of believers is the second part of our general commission. In 1 Corinthians chapter 12, we have a vivid description of how the Lord sees His church. He likens it to the human body, which has many diverse members. While verse 12 asserts that we're all members of one body, the universal body of believers, the passage also mentions that we need to be part of a local group of Christians. Verse 18 states that God will personally place each of us in a specific area of His body. We will always live out our place in a local body. As we live out our place, both we and the local body of which we are a part will operate a higher level. This will be true for the overall body as more of us find and fill our places.

God indicates that, as in the human body, there should be no divisiveness between members. No one believer is more important than any other. No member should exalt himself or degrade others. Clearly spoken, we need one another:

> *If the foot says, "Because I am not a hand, I am not a part of the body," it is not for this reason any the less a part of the body. And if the ear says, "Because I am not an eye, I am not a part of the body," it is not for this reason any the less a part of the body. If the whole body were an eye, where would the hearing be? If the whole were hearing, where would the sense of smell be?...If they were all one member, where would the body be? But now there are many members, but one body. And the*

eye cannot say to the hand, "I have no need of you"; or again the head to the feet, "I have no need of you."…There may be no division in the body, but that the members may have the same care for one another. And if one member suffers, all the members suffer with it; if one member is honored, all the members rejoice with it. Now you are Christ's body, and individually members of it.   (1 Corinthians 12:15–17, 19–21, 25–27)

While this analogy is encouraging, God also gives us clear instructions on how to daily and effectively live it out. The New Testament gives thirty specific orders that direct believers on how to live as loving members of Christ's church. Following these orders requires that we establish deep relationships rooted in love and trust. These relationships demand time and effort to build, which is impossible for a person who is constantly on the move from fellowship group to group.

The following is what I call the "checklist of relationship success." If we can fulfill this list, we are well on our way to living the life Christ meant for each of us to enjoy. I personally believe that every Christian should be part of a small, home-based group of other believers with whom he or she can live out the following list. This allows for interaction, accountability, and unconditional love. I challenge you to become part of such a meaningful group—for your sake and for theirs. If the thought of it seems hard for you, push through your fears and dislikes and do it anyway. You'll find a richer life and closer friendships.

Checklist of Relationship Success

1. *"**Love** one another"* (John 13:34–35).

2. Be *"**members** one of another"* (Romans 12:5).

3. *"Be **devoted** to one another"* (Romans 12:10).

4. *"Outdo one another in showing **honor**"* (Romans 12:10 ESV).

5. "**Rejoice** with one another." (See Romans 12:15.)

6. "**Weep** with one another." (See Romans. 12:15.)

7. "Have the **same mind** toward one another." (See Romans 12:16.)

8. "Do **not judge** one another." (See Romans 14:13.)

9. "*Accept one another*" (Romans 15:7).

10. **Build up** one another. (See Romans 15:14.)

11. "*Greet one another*" (Romans 16:16).

12. "*Wait for one another*" (1 Corinthians 11:33).

13. "*Care for one another*" (1 Corinthians 12:25).

14. "*Serve one another*" (Galatians 5:13).

15. "*Bear one another's burdens*" (Galatians 6:2).

16. "*Be **kind** to one another*" (Ephesians 4:32).

17. "**Forgive** one another." (See Ephesians 4:32.)

18. "**Submit** to one another." (See Ephesians 5:21.)

19. "**Counsel** one another." (See Colossians 3:16.)

20. "**Bear** with one another." (See Colossians 3:13.)

21. "*Encourage one another*" (1 Thessalonians 5:11).

22. "**Stir up** one another." (See Hebrews 10:24.)

23. "*Do **not speak evil** against one another*" (James 4:11 ESV).

24. "*Do **not grumble** against one another*" (James 5:9 ESV).

25. "**Confess** your faults to one another." (See James 5:16.)

26. "*Pray for one another*" (James 5:16).

27. "*Be **hospitable** to one another*" (1 Peter 4:9).

28. **Minister** to one another. (See 1 Peter 4:10.)

29. "Be clothed with **humility** toward one another." (See 1 Peter 5:5.)

30. *"Fellowship with one another"* (1 John 1:7).

COMMISSION #3: LIGHT IT UP

The third and final part of the general commission to believers is that of sharing our kingdom life with others who have never met Jesus. This is a major aspect of letting our light shine in a dark world. It is known as "being a witness." In Jesus' final words before His ascension, He said:

All authority has been given to Me in heaven and on earth. Go therefore and make disciples of all the nations, baptizing them in the name of the Father and the Son and the Holy Spirit, teaching them to observe all that I commanded you; and lo, I am with you always, even to the end of the age.
(Matthew 28:18–20)

And He said to them, "Go into all the world and preach the gospel to all creation. He who has believed and has been baptized shall be saved; but he who has disbelieved shall be condemned. These signs will accompany those who have believed: in My name they will cast out demons, they will speak with new tongues; they will pick up serpents, and if they drink any deadly poison, it shall not hurt them; they will lay hands on the sick, and they will recover." (Mark 16:15–18)

But you will receive power when the Holy Spirit has come upon you; and you shall be My witnesses both in Jerusalem, and in all Judea and Samaria, and even to the remotest part of the earth. (Acts 1:8)

These verses explain that *we* are to preach, teach, administer God's healing power, deliver the captives of Satan, and baptize those who believe. There's nothing passive about this. It's aggressive in the sense that we are to boldly reach out to people who don't know Jesus. We do not beat them up about their sin but inspire them with the truth of God's love for them. We let them see His love in our daily lives, then share the gospel with them when they open the door for us to do so.

My friend Dr. Timothy Johns calls this the "Prayer-Care-Share" method of evangelism. Pray for the person to be open to hearing the gospel. Express your loving care for them in some way. Then share the gospel when they ask you about your life and love for them. It's pretty powerful!

Billions of people are just as we were before we met Christ, and they need what we have. Sharing our faith in Jesus is our privilege, and it is the main reason we are left on this planet after we make Jesus the Master of our lives. It's up to us—the living church of Jesus Christ—and us alone.

> For "WHOEVER WILL CALL ON THE NAME OF THE LORD WILL BE SAVED." *How then will they call on Him in whom they have not believed? How will they believe in Him whom they have not heard? And how will they hear without a preacher?...So faith comes from hearing, and hearing by the word of Christ.*
> (Romans 10:13–14, 17)

Countless books have been written about witnessing. Courses in personal evangelism are easy to find. But if you want a clear, simple method of being a successful witness for Christ, remember this phrase: *Find a need and meet it, with loving-kindness, compassion, and the power of the Holy Spirit!*

With the power of God at your disposal, you can transcend the impossible. All you need to do is apply it. Do everything within your ability to educate yourself on sharing the gospel and making disciples. Witnessing is the most exciting and rewarding element of the Christian life.

And Jesus said to him, "If You can?" All things are possible to
him who believes.   (Mark 9:23)

Letting your light shine before men is your fundamental purpose as a part of the universal body of Christ. Each of us is to
take that truth and daily apply it to an ever-darkening world. This
requires each of us to buckle down to the task of maintaining the
lordship of Christ in our lives through daily worship, Bible study,
and obedience. We must find our place in a local body of believers
and live out our personal visions. Our lives must become examples
of living to give. Our light shines as we witness about the glories of
our God and King. Boldly yet humbly displaying Christ to a hurting world is God's plan for all believers.

FINAL THOUGHTS

It's amazing to me that God, the Creator of everything in this
universe, would trust such vital work to fragile, vulnerable creatures
as human beings. But that's the miracle of God—that He lives His
life through us so we're not dependent on our own abilities. Yes, the
general purpose for Christ's church is enormous, but it's one every
believer can and must accept. We can do it. He will help us.

> "Even if all…needs are satisfied, we may still often (if not
> always) expect that a new discontent and restlessness will
> soon develop, unless the individual is doing what he is
> fitted for. A musician must make music, an artist must
> paint, a poet must write, if he is to be ultimately happy.
> What a man can be, he must be."
> —*Abraham Maslow*

My goal with this chapter has been to inspire you to believe
that you are valuable and unique and that you and your destiny

matter in God's kingdom and so in this world. This probaby has sparked some questions for you, such as, "How do I actually discover the purpose for my life?" First, you need to understand that you have already been endowed with many incredible tools you'll need for that journey.

4

WHAT'S MY MIX?

*"As each one has received a special gift, employ it in serving
one another as good stewards of the manifold grace of God."*
—1 Peter 4:10

The Lord in His infinite wisdom has chosen to give every one of
His children personal gifts. Each gift has a specific function and
place in the overall picture of His will for this age. These gifts are
given to assist the individual believer as he or she lives out God's
ordained purpose. In Paul's letter to the Romans, he states:

> *For just as we have many members in one body and all the
> members do not have the same function, so we, who are many,
> are one body in Christ, and individually members one of
> another. Since we have gifts that differ according to the grace
> given to us, each of us is to exercise them accordingly.*
>
> (Romans 12:4–6)

According to these verses, the main reason individual members of the church are given gifts is to serve one another. Our
personal purpose will be enhanced by the gifts entrusted to us by
the Lord. By effectively using our gifts, we'll enhance the overall

effectiveness of Christ's body. The sharing of our gifts with one another will complete the body of which we are to be a part.

"We all have some gifts, but we don't have most."
—*Steven K. Scott*

A MIXED BAG

Another aspect of these gifts is that they help you serve others more effectively. By skillfully operating in your gifts, you will enhance your relationships with your friends, family, community members, and possibly more. And if you can help others find and use their special gifts, you and everyone else they interact with will benefit even more.

There's a wonderful give-and-take that occurs when we use our gifts. My gifts will complement yours, and yours will complement mine. Although I'm definitely not gifted in math, my wife is, and therefore she handles the bookkeeping. Where she lacks in understanding, such as knowing the difference between e-books and social media, I take over that chore. In a community we can all function in a similar manner, with each person supplying what's needed at the moment, as it fits his or her giftings. No person's gifts should be seen solely for self-gratification. We are to share our gifts as freely as we have received them.

From whom the whole body, being fitted and held together by what every joint supplies, according to the proper working of each individual part, causes the growth of the body for the building up of itself in love. (Ephesians 4:16)

Whether it be our natural gifts, our spiritual gifts, or even our intellectual ones, all are meant to strengthen and complete the body of Christ.

"The measure of life is not its duration, but its donation."
—*Peter Marshall*

MAKE A LIST

To the best of your ability, before you read further, make a list of all the gifts you believe you have. This list will be crucial to your understanding and accomplishing your purpose in this life. Your gifts are a major part of your personal "tool box." Perhaps you have gifts in the major areas of life, such as physical, financial, social, spiritual, or intellectual. If you have a *Purpose Master Planner*, find the "Gifts and Skills" list and fill it out to the best of your ability. If there are gifts you feel you possess that aren't listed on the worksheet, by all means add them. This list will help you to understanding and accomplish the purpose and destiny God has prepared for you.

PHYSICAL GIFTS

This category of gifts includes the physical abilites people possess, including talents, expertise, or above-average control of one's body. Activities such as running, jumping, throwing, and swimming are good examples. A gifted person would find such actions simple to learn and easy to perfect. You know the guy who possesses physical gifts—the first time he picks up a baseball, he's striking out most of the best players in town! Or the girl who buys a tennis racket one day, and by the following week she's ready for tournaments! Are these gross exaggerations? Certainly! But to someone who throws a frisbee like a shot put, it seems all too close to reality. A gifted athlete stands out.

Not all natural gifts come under the heading of sports or athletics, however. Such gifts as singing; playing the piano or other musical instruments; drawing; sculpting; acting; and even miming also fit under this heading. These gifts are easily recognized, as well. Many can sing, but few have a three- or four-octave range. A multitude may play piano, but few perform in a concert at Carnegie Hall. Again, a gifted person is spotted easily among the average.

INTELLECTUAL GIFTS

Intellectual gifts are primarily concerned with our mental abilites. I'm not talking here about mind-over-matter ability, by which someone seems to bend spoons and move small objects. Mental gifts relate to the above-average ability to understand and apply what we learn intellectually.

We all know someone who excels beyond reason in such areas as mathematics or physics. Perhaps you personally have the capacity to remember the smallest detail of a book you've read or some event you witnessed. Another person may understand the workings of electricity to the point that he or she thoroughly confuses the average listener while trying to explain it's power. I'm not talking about a genius, but anyone who just "get's it" much easier than the average person and can apply what he or she learns with little effort. The person just have a knack for it; he's gifted.

I've never had a problem with memorizing anything. Most of my academic career was spent on athletic fields instead of in study hall, because I could remember most information I read and reviewed once or twice. Although this was a valuable asset at exam time, it made my school years pretty boring. It's not much fun throwing a football to yourself while everyone else is pouring over test materials.

But even with this gift, I was never good at some subjects. I was always frustrated by math problems with equations more advanced than adding, substracting, multiplying, and dividing. Memorizing math concepts for exams was never a problem, but applying them in the checkout line—no way!

So whether you are a singer, musician, communicator, carpenter, mechanic, artist, designer, tight end, outfielder, writer, or certified public accountant, you are meant to use your gifts to bless both you and those around you. At the end of this chapter, we'll take a close look at how we use and abuse of our gifts.

"SUPER"-NATURAL GIFTS

A person's natural gifts are often increased after they are born again in Christ. For example, before I became a Christian, I was interested in sports. In high school, I tried out for the football team, the basketball team, and the track team. Sometimes I proved to be average, but more often, mediocre. Organized sports and I gelled like water and oil. All I received for my anemic high school athletic career was two points scored playing basketball, two wins out of thirty-six football games, one first-place ribbon (and a few second and third) for pole vaulting on the track team, two brain concussions, a cracked shin, a couple of broken fingers, and a broken knee that required a hip-to-ankle cast! To say that I was *not* gifted is to overstate the obvious.

But in 1971, a phenomenal thing began to occur. Shortly after giving my life to the Lord in the fall of that year, I took up karate. I excelled! Two years later, I joined the Florida State University Flying High Circus. Within a few short weeks, I was publicly performing in several acts, including trapeze and the very difficult slack wire, which normally took a person months to have show-ready. My fellow circus performers were astounded by the ease with which I acquired these skills and with the rapid development of my chosen acts. I became a top performer, and I went on to master almost every skill in the show, from flying and catching on the trapeze to juggling and balancing on wire and teeterboards.

What made the difference between the mediocrity of my high school years and the meteoric rise of my abilities in college? My only answer and my firm belief is that the Holy Spirit took my natural abilities and added supernatural abundance to them. His motives weren't for my personal pleasure alone but for the strengthening of the church and ministry to unbelievers. Although it took me several years to realize that, I eventually aligned my motives with His, and Circus Alleluia was born to proclaim Jesus Christ as Lord across North America. Gifted and not, we will find new power when Christ gains full control of our life.

SPIRITUAL GIFTS

Spiritual gifts are bestowed upon believers to assist them in the overall function of the entire body of Christ. Does this sound like an echo of our discussion of natural gifts? Well, there is one major difference—the Holy Spirit. Natural gifts are affected by genetics as well as God's pleasure, but spiritual gifts are specifically distributed by the Holy Spirit and are not bound by a person's physical abilities or ancestry. The only prerequisite for being given spiritual gifts by the Holy Spirit of God is that a person is born again through the resurrection power of Jesus Christ. Until the Holy Spirit has been given the opportunity to dwell within a person, He won't release the spiritual gifts in the way He desires.

I believe that many people are given spiritual gifts at conception. However, unless a person is born again by God's Holy Spirit, those gifts in him can be perverted and manipulated by the devil, as in the case of "psychic" phenomenon. Although psychics may be sincere in their desire to help others, they are merely taking the very people they wish to aid further from the Lord, who is the only one who can truly meet their needs. But such manipulated gifts can never match the Holy Spirit's gifts for His people.

The spiritual gifts that the Lord imparts to us actually have the power to transcend the laws and understanding of the natural world around us. They are given to allow believers to perform specific acts and to live out otherwise impossible assignments dictated by their position in Christ's body. These gifts are listed in several books of the New Testament. Not everyone will experience every gift, and some believers may possess more gifts than others, just as with natural gifts. The point, however, is not how many gifts we have, but what we do with the gifts that we have received.

> *Now concerning spiritual gifts, brethren, I do not want you to be unaware.* (1 Corinthians 12:1)

The apostle Paul expresses his concern that believers must not be ignorant or unaware of the spiritual gifts God has entrusted to them. That includes you and me. The Lord, through Paul, goes on to illuminate several of the gifts to which He refers. Those gifts fall into three distinct categories:

1. Gifts of the Holy Spirit
2. Motivational gifts
3. Ministerial gifts

The first category of gifts is so named because the Holy Spirit is specifically mentioned as the One who decides when and through whom these gifts will be activated. Also, these particular gifts are purely *supernatural*; they are activated solely by the power of the Holy Spirit working through an individual. They are usually given at a specific moment to meet a particular need. This is in contrast to the motivational and ministerial gifts, which operate in an ongoing fashion.

The gifts of the Holy Spirit listed below, as well as those under the other two headings just mentioned, will be given only a small explanation here. My intention is to share the basics of their workings so that you may take this information and seek further insight on your own through other publications, meditation, and prayer. These brief summaries will, however, provide valuable insight into the spiritual gifts with which the Lord has specifically blessed you with.

GIFTS OF THE HOLY SPIRIT

These nine gifts are given by the Holy Spirit to whom He wills and when He wills. The key to operating in these gifts is to know how they are received. The obvious need, then, is to know when the gifts are operating and how to utilize them. Although some people experience certain physical feelings when the Holy Spirit is operating one of the gifts through them, such feelings are neither common nor necessary.

The only way a believer can have a clear understanding that the Holy Spirit is moving upon him in the area of one of these gifts is to establish clear, two-way communication. This communication comes only through daily time with God. (We will discuss the language of the Holy Spirit in a later chapter, for unless you understand His language, your learning to flow with Him in the area of these gifts will be greatly hindered.)

Having said that, I must also say that the Lord can drop any spiritual gift He likes upon anyone at anytime, regardless of whether the person has asked for it or has a clue how it works! I've met many believers with extraordinary gifts of the Holy Spirit who never knew there was such a thing until the gift suddenly "turned on" one day. This is the exception and not the rule, however. Those who experience such gift "downloads" can get into trouble with their newfound abilities and need solid, experienced leaders around them to help them avoid the pitfalls. This seemed especially prevalent in the prophetic gifts during the late 1980s and early 1990s, when so much of this was not fully understood by church leaders.

> *Now there are varieties of gifts, but the same Spirit. And there are varieties of ministries, and the same Lord. There are varieties of effects, but the same God who works all things in all persons. But to each one is given the manifestation of the Spirit for the common good. For to one is given the word of*

*wisdom through the Spirit, and to another the word of knowl-
edge according to the same Spirit; to another faith by the same
Spirit, and to another gifts of healing by the one Spirit, and
to another the effecting of miracles, and to another prophecy, and to another the distinguishing of spirits, to another
various kinds of tongues, and to another the interpretation of
tongues. But one and the same Spirit works all these things,
distributing to each one individually just as He wills.*

(1 Corinthians 12:4–11)

WORD OF WISDOM

Wisdom is the ability to use what we know to the fullest
extent. This gift is a combination of the knowledge at hand and
the supernatural, overall understanding possessed by the Holy
Spirit for meeting the particular need of the situation or individual. It brings solutions. It's not dependent on the knowledge of the
person administering the gift. I've marveled at the words that have
come from my mouth for people I was ministering to when this
gift is operating through me. There's no way I could have known or
thought of the answers and solutions I was giving. This gift brings
the specific information to meet a need.

WORD OF KNOWLEDGE

A word of knowledge is specific information, which one has
no natural way of knowing, that is revealed to the believer to meet
a very specific need in the body of Christ or in an individual's life.
Often this gift is found working with the gifts of miracles and
healing. The Holy Spirit has given me such words of knowledge
literally thousands of times over my ministerial career, and I find
that it's a powerful blessing to recipients.

Once, while praying for the sick after one of our circus performances, the words "cystic fibrosis" came to my mind. I had
never heard those words before, but I knew it must be a disease

of some sort. I called for anyone with such a disease to come forward, and only one young boy ventured forth from the audience of several hundred people. When I rebuked the disease in the name of Jesus Christ, the Lord instantly healed the boy of cystic fibrosis and two other diseases, which was later confirmed by his doctors. That word of knowledge was given to allow the gift of healing to be administered. God is so amazing!

FAITH

The gift of faith is the supernatural ability to believe beyond all doubt that the Lord will do as He said He would. This ability allows the recipient to stand firm in the face of what, in the natural realm, seems to be completely impossible. It can be both long-range and short-range in function.

One morning, I was awakened by my wife to see a tornado heading straight for our house. While still shaking the sleep from my head, I pointed my finger at the giant and commanded it to pull back into the clouds and be gone. There was no fear or doubt on my part, and the tornado instantly obeyed! Meg added, "And you can't hurt anyone, either!" The tornado touched down in a trailer park less than a mile away, but it managed only to knock down some trees and tear off some siding. No one was injured in the slightest! From Bible study, I knew that I possessed authority over the weather. The faith to remove that storm hinged on a knowledge of the Lord's Word already in my spirit. The power came through the gift of God enlarging my faith to the capacity necessary for that moment.

HEALING

A person with this gift allows the Lord to pour His power through him to heal someone else's physical body without natural aids, such as in the case of the boy with cystic fibrosis. However, this gift can also be given directly to the person who needs healing, without a person who administers the gift. There are no limits to the power of this gift to heal the human body as well as the human soul.

MIRACLES

Miracles defy all natural laws and can actually change the structure or course of nature itself. The dismissal of the tornado mentioned above was a result of the gift of miracles operating with the gift of faith. Often, there is a form of creative power unleashed in the delivery of a miracle, such as the regeneration of body parts or the raising of someone from the dead, but it can also pertain to material provision, such as the feeding of the five thousand by Jesus. Miracles are normally associated with instantaneous results.

DISCERNING OF SPIRITS

This gift enables a believer to know with certainty the type of spirit behind certain situations, behaviors, or actions. It's often used to discern demonic activity, but it can also be used to confirm the presence and the will of God. In the case of demonic force, the actual name of the spirit may be given. At other times, it may simply be a "yes or no" discernment of what the source or activity is.

A few years ago, a man came to the church where I was an associate pastor. From his talk, he sounded very spiritual. My spirit, however, was never comfortable around him. Many people thought he was a great humanitarian and servant, but I just couldn't buy it for some reason. Within a few weeks after his arrival, he began to create much division among our congregants. Eventually, he was asked to leave our fellowship because he would not submit to the elders' authority and instruction concerning his conduct. My uneasiness was a form of discerning of spirits. The man was not motivated by the Lord but by spirits of lust for control and power over others. The Holy Spirit revealed this to me through my uneasiness to confirm what was eventually brought to light.

TONGUES

The gift of tongues is given to a believer to bring a message to the church or to an individual. It is a language the believer has never learned and does not understand, even when he speaks it. This gift of tongues is always to be followed by the gift of interpretation, so that those who hear it may receive the interpretation of the message. This gift of tongues is not to be confused with the tongues, or prayer language, given to believers when they receive the baptism in the Holy Spirit. That gift of tongues is totally personal and can be utilized by the believer at any moment he or she desires, without specific unction from the Holy Spirit. The gift of tongues mentioned in 1 Corinthians 12 is a *specific* urging of the Holy Spirit for a *specific* reason at a *specific* time.

INTERPRETATION OF TONGUES

This gift is given to interpret a message given in tongues into the language of those who hear it. Paul clearly stated in 1 Corinthians 14 that tongues without interpretation does the body of Christ no good, even though it edifies the person who speaks merely because of his obedience. Interpretation immediately follows a message in tongues, and it may come through the same person who spoke it, although that will not always be the case. It is not a word-for-word translation but an interpretation, so the amount of spoken words may not match what is said in tongues.

PROPHECY

The gift of prophecy is a specific word given to the believer from the Lord concerning a specific event, situation, person, or group. Often it relates to future events. It may be directive, corrective, or simply informative, but it will most often be exhortive, consoling, or comforting. It can be metaphoric or even pictorial. Normally there should be a confirmation and acceptance of the prophecy by a spiritual leader present, or it should be presented to such leaders before any action is taken.

MOTIVATIONAL GIFTS

The second gift category we will look at is motivational gifts, or action-initiating gifts. These are the gifts that spur Christians to action, usually in a service-oriented way. Motivational gifts tend to function on a daily basis, rather than at specific moments, as directed by the Holy Spirit. All believers will have one or more of these gifts operating in their lives at one time or another. To list these motivational gifts, we must look at 1 Corinthians 12 and Romans 12.

Since we have gifts that differ according to the grace given to us, each of us is to exercise them accordingly: if prophecy, according to the proportion of his faith; if service, in his serving; or he who teaches, in his teaching; or he who exhorts, in his exhortation; he who gives, with liberality; he who leads, with diligence; he who shows mercy, with cheerfulness.

(Romans 12:6–8)

And God has appointed in the church, first apostles, second prophets, third teachers, then miracles, then gifts of healings, helps, administrations, various kinds of tongues.

(1 Corinthians 12:28)

PROPHECY

This motivational gift is not to be confused with the Holy Spirit's gift of prophecy. The Holy Spirit's gift of prophecy mentioned in 1 Corinthians 12 is bestowed for *specific* instances, as the Spirit dictates; the motivational gift of prophecy is an ongoing gift that is a regular part of the person's spiritual life. As a part of the believer's personality, it is the ability to see into a situation or a person's life and bring a message from the Lord that pertains to a need or problem. It may also pertain to upcoming events. The person with this gift may not necessarily be a prophet; yet he or she can be just as accurate in his or her prophecies.

SERVICE

This gift motivates the believer to serve the brethren in various practical ways. These people are always the ones cleaning up after a group function or taking food to the needy. They are seemingly *driven* to serve in some way or another and are happiest when doing just that.

TEACHING

The gift of teaching causes the believer to be constantly looking for the exactness of truth in God's Word. The person with this gift desires to present the pure Word of God in a way that will benefit the church. The ability to place things in a precept-by-precept, point-by-point outline is a good indication that this gift is in operation within you. However, having this gift does not necessarily mean that you are anointed with the ministry of a teacher, as will be explained under the "Ministry Gifts" heading.

EXHORTATION

A person with the gift of exhortation will inspire, uplift, comfort, excite, and motivate the body of Christ. Believers with this gift are constantly edifying others and encouraging them to do great things for the Lord.

GIVING

This gift motivates believers to give of their natural and material resources for the benefit of others. They enjoy giving in every area and desire to move others to do so. Quite often, these people are skilled at producing or raising finances for specific needs or ministries.

LEADERSHIP

The gift of leadership enables the believer to organize and set goals for others and then direct those people in accomplishing those goals. This person will keep the ball rolling and will help everyone work together toward the common end. They usually lead by example and not merely by giving orders.

MERCY

This gift will move the believer with compassion and empathy toward those in great personal distress. They will perform the necessary tasks to help hurting people find relief. These people are very loving and self-sacrificing.

HELPS

The gift of helps motivates the believer to pour his time, efforts, gifts, and talents into the lives and ministries of others. They enjoy assisting others. The majority of believers are called to this gift, and all are to operate in it to some extent—even if just in the local church.

ADMINISTRATIONS

The person with this gift will understand the goals—both short-term and long-term—of a group and will be involved in planning and execution them at the leadership level. This is a much-needed gift for the majority of ministries; most are founded and led by visionaries who aren't detail-oriented. My experience has shown that the strongest and most effective organizations have excellent administrators on their teams.

MINISTRY GIFTS

And He gave some as apostles, and some as prophets, and some as evangelists, and some as pastors and teachers, for the equipping of the saints for the work of service, to the building up of the body of Christ; until we all attain to the unity of the faith, and of the knowledge of the Son of God, to a mature man, to the measure of the stature which belongs to the fullness of Christ.   (Ephesians 4:11–13)

The third category of spiritual gifts is often called the "five-fold" ministry gifts because there are five of them. They are given to certain believers called by God to equip the saints for the work of ministry. Although attributes of these gifts may be enjoyed by many believers, this gift category is primarily for those with a lifetime call. Christians possessing these gifts are the trainers, coaches, and drill sergeants of God's army.

The majority of Christ's body will *not* have these special gifts. If all were trainers, there'd be no one to be trained. All believers, however, should have a knowledge of these five gifts so that they can receive from the anointed folk who possess them. Note that there are levels of anointing or ability associated with these gifts. For example, some may function on a small local scale while others with the same gift function on a global scale.

APOSTLE

An apostle, or a "sent one," is an authoritative figure usually recognized by several church bodies rather than one specific church. This person will often plant new churches and then oversee the spiritual workings of those local bodies. The apostle will speak into the leadership in those churches. The apostle, along with the prophet, is said to be the foundation on which the church is built, thereby contributing to the overall anointing, kingdom view, and understanding of the Lord's will. (See Ephesians 2:20.)

PROPHET

A prophet is both the friend and the voice of God to His people in a profound and consistent way. The gift of prophecy operates in his or her ministry with great accuracy, although New Testament instruction demands that even a seasoned prophet's words must be judged by others. (See 1 Corinthians 14:29–33.) A prophet speaks in a way that convicts as well as edifies. He may tell of future events concerning the world and the church, or he may reveal the meaning of past and present events. His attitude is usually one of absolute submission to God. He is the messenger but not necessarily the one to interpret the message or administer its fulfillment, which is why this person should to be partnered with an apostle.

EVANGELIST

This gift allows the believer to share the gospel with people under an anointing of God that often brings unusual conviction and conversion among the hearers. The evangelist is successful in leading many to salvation in one-on-one settings and possibly in mass-meeting situations. He will be consumed by the desire to tell people about Christ and to train and exhort other believers to do the same.

PASTOR

A pastor is a shepherd to a specific group of brethren. He or she has an ongoing understanding of and concern for the needs of a church. A pastor helps teach, comfort, direct, and correct the congregation to meet those needs. This is usually a long-range position lived out with one church body, but not always. A pastor must surround him- or herself with other ministry gifts to be able to sustain the weight of the needs of the church. Pastors are not always the lead minister of a church group, nor do they need to be; but they are absolutely necessary for its growth and well-being.

TEACHER

This gift is different from the motivational gift of teaching in that it is a lifetime spiritual leadership calling, not a gift that is used occasionally. This gift enables a believer to acquire and then share with the church in-depth truths of the kingdom of God in a systematic and logical way. His or her goal is to ensure that hearers both learn and apply what is taught. He delights in using every available circumstance as a tool or example to share a biblical truth with anyone who will listen. The teacher usually sees every revelation as one to be taught to the body of Christ.

OUR RESPONSIBILITY

Each of us has received one or more of the motivational and/ or ministry gifts listed in this chapter. The gifts of the Holy Spirit are given at the discretion of the Lord for a specific time and event. But as with anything given freely by the Lord, we must accept responsibility for exercising the gift and producing fruit. God expects us to cultivate a desire for our gifts, actually striving to operate in the gifts that are considered greater than the others. (See 1 Corinthians 12:31–14:1.)

The Lord even takes the point a step further by prodding us to stir up or rekindle the gifts within us that may have become dormant. (See 2 Timothy 1:6.) And, just in case there's a hardhead in the camp (such as yours truly!), 1 Timothy 4:14 exhorts us to make sure that neglecting our gifts is *never* an option. As explained throughout the Epistles, the responsibility of using our gifts—be they spiritual or natural—quite plainly is ours, not God's.

Think about it. What giver is held responsible for the gift once it has been given? No one, obviously. Furthermore, what giver isn't frustrated when the gift is left unused by the receiver? Clearly, the Father trusts His children to be good stewards. (See Matthew 25:14–30.)

It's not the number of gifts we possess that determines our reward, but what we *do* with what we're given. If we're faithful to do our best with our gifts, then there will be a reward for us. As has been said, "The pay is the same," regardless of your assignment within God's kingdom. It is the person who does *nothing* with the gift granted to him who will be found lacking. If we fail to use our gifts for the kingdom of God, neither we nor those around us will enjoy the fruit of them.

I trained for years to acquire the skill necessary to climb a ladder while balancing it on a slack wire, which has the thickness of a pencil. Lack of practice took its toll more than once after a misplaced step or an overcompensation in balance—usually with quite painful results. Just as my skills had to be kept sharp through investing time in rigorous practice sessions to avoid dangerous accidents, so our spiritual gifts must be kept "sharp."

> "Man discovers his own wealth when
> God comes to ask gifts of him."
> —*Rabindranath Tagore*

The gifts the Lord has endowed you with are for His glory and for meeting the needs of people, often within His body. As each of us finds our specific gifts and begins to live them out, the church will be strengthened and the world will be forced to take notice. *These gifts are for giving away.* They are for each of us to use to assist one another in our purposes in life. As we find and develop our individual purposes, our spiritual and natural gifts will come more and more into play. You *are* gifted!

SKILLS

Let me share a word about the difference between gifts and skills. A skilled person may have little or no gifting in his skill area, and a gifted person may have little or no skill in his area of gifting. We've all observed highly skilled athletes or performers who had been cut from their team or group in the early years of their quest due to a lack of talent. Furthermore, we have seen gifted players who have never risen to the heights they are capable of reaching because they had not disciplined themselves to perfect their skill. Why? Because there is no *desire*.

Desire is the burning force within us that compels us to go on in the face of seemingly insurmountable odds. A man with desire will overcome every obstacle. Every conqueror, every inventor, every explorer has experienced this type of motivating force. When someone has a burning desire to learn, to excel, to go beyond the average and even beyond the limits of his or her own ability, greatness is born. That is where desire shines brightest.

Basketball star Michael Jordan had a desire to be a great ballplayer from a young age. But he was so bad at the game that he was cut from his high school team in the tenth grade. He had a choice to make—give in to defeat or fuel the fire of desire even more. He chose the fire! His high school coach offered to train Michael before school every day so that he could make the team in his junior year. From that point on, Michael never looked back. He went on to a renowned college career and then on to the pros. Here is what he accomplished.

+ Rookie of the Year (1985)
+ All-NBA Second Team (1985)
+ NBA Defensive Player of the Year (1987–98)
+ Six-time NBA champion (1991–93, 1996–98)
+ Three-time NBA All-Star Game MVP (1988, 1996, 1998)
+ Ten-time All-NBA First Team (1987–93, 1996–98)
+ Nine-time All-Defensive First Team (1988–93, 1996–98)
+ Fourteen-time All-Star; All-Star MVP (1988, 1996, 1998)
+ One of 50 Greatest Players in NBA History (1996)
+ Two-time Olympic gold medalist (1984, 1992)

Was Michael the most gifted basketball player? Many will debate that, including Michael. What is *not* up for debate is the intensity of the desire he displayed throughout his career. He worked harder to perfect his skills than almost any other player. His work ethic was unequaled. He was often the last man off the court during practice, leaving others shake their heads at his drive to improve.

Skill is not given to anyone; it's acquired. It's not dependent upon gifting but is definitely helped by it. In my own life, I've found that skills come with the decision to go get them and the desire to do what it takes to own them. I believe that if a Christian is given a gift, it's his or her duty to turn that gift into a skill for the glory of God and the helping of others. I hope you agree with that. I hope you live it.

FINAL THOUGHTS

*For I long to see you so that I may **impart** some spiritual **gift** to you, that you may be **established**.*   (Romans 1:11)

Paul's longing to impart gifts to the church in Rome wasn't so much for the gift itself, but that through the gift, those believers would be established in their faith. He understood that the person who was in step with the gifts of God's Spirit would be in a position for victory. This is my prayer for you, as well.

When you discover and begin to live within the realm of the gifts God has entrusted to you as a believer, you'll become established within His body. Through those gifts, you'll tap into the power of God to live out your particular purpose, thereby helping to fulfill the purpose of your local church and the body of Christ at large. Discover your personal gifts and how to practically use them in your daily life. You *are* gifted! Now let's talk more about the power of desire.

5

WHAT DO I
REALLY WANT?

"Lord, grant that I may always
desire more than I can accomplish!"
—*Michelangelo*

*"Delight yourself in the LORD; and He will give you the
desires of your heart."*
—Psalm 37:4

Desire means to crave or to long for something. It's an inner motivating, propelling, energizing dynamo. As I mentioned in the last chapter in our discussion of skills, desire can drive men to accomplish greatness or to die pursuingsomething that may not even exist. The Scripture above shows us how desire relates to the nature of God. Psalm 37:4 implies that God will give us not only desires by placing them in our hearts but also the ability to fulfill those desires. To give us the desires of our hearts is no small gift.

Desire is a powerful force in the life of one who understands how to use it. I've counseled and spoken with countless people who struggle with desire. Obviously there are instinctive desires, such as human desires for food and shelter. But what about the desires for success and achievement? What about financial desires? Social desires? Material desires? Career, education, or family desires? I believe that God wants us to have the desires of our hearts—as long as they are the desires *He* gives to us.

God will never give you a desire that is not in line with His Word. He's not looking for opportunities to trip us up. He longs to give us what He knows will give us the most joy, just as any Father would. He wants us to enjoy our lives. He knows exactly what we can and cannot handle. So, the desires He places in us and then helps us to fulfill are the best we could ever hope for.

THE DREAMS AND DESIRES LIST

What would you love to do? What gives you the most joy? What is the most fulfilling and rewarding thing that you do now? Is there something you really want to do but have never done? If you could work any job, what would you do? What job would you do even if you did not get paid for it? What are your dreams?

If you've never asked yourself these questions, or if you never answered them honestly, I challenge you to do so now. In the *Purpose Master Planner*, there's a worksheet entitled "Dreams and Desires." You'll notice that I've listed six specific headings, which I call "life areas," under which you can place your dreams and desires. These areas are the framework of your life, the pillars if you will. If you don't have a *Purpose Master Planner*, just write your dreams and desires on a piece of notebook paper. Let me explain the life areas a bit, as we'll refer to them in almost every chapter from now on.

Each life area is a category falls into one or more of the three parts of man—spirit, soul, and body. (See 1 Thessalonians 5:23.) I'll discuss the several subheadings more in-depth in chapter 10, "God Goals." Look over this list and memorize it as best as you can. Keep yourself tuned in to just these six areas, and you'll maintain a very productive life. Know them and make them the primary focus of your daily disciplines.

1. **Spirit:** "If you walk in the Spirit, you will not do the deeds of the flesh." (See Galatians 5:16.) This area covers everything connected with your growth as a Christian through your personal relationship with God.

2. **Intellect:** *"We have the mind of Christ"* (1 Corinthians 2:16) and are *"transformed by the renewing of* [our] *mind"* (Romans 12:2). This area concerns your mental capacities, such as learning, thinking, reasoning, knowledge, understanding, and wisdom.

3. **Personality:** *"But the fruit of the Spirit is love, joy, peace, patience, kindness, goodness, faithfulness, gentleness, self control…"* (Galatians 5:22–23). This area deals with who you are—your attitudes, emotions, act/react inclinations, confidence, fears, skills, gifts, and motivations.

4. **Physical:** *"Your body is the temple of the Holy Spirit"* (1 Corinthians 6:19). *"But I discipline my body and make it my slave"* (1 Corinthians 9:27). This area refers to your physical body—your health, your activities (such as sports or travel), and the care of your body.

5. **Social:** *"Love one another, even as I have loved you"* (John 13:34). This area includes all your human relationships and related activities with your family, spouse, coworkers, persons with whom you associate in organizations or in ministry to others, and those in your local church.

6. **Financial:** *"Riches and honor are with me* [wisdom], *enduring wealth and righteousness"* (Proverbs 8:18). This area has to do with wealth and your production, such as your career or occupation, and the expenditure, giving, and investment of material goods throughout your life.

Look at your list of dreams. Place at least one dream and desire in each appropriate life area. Record as many dreams and desires as you wish. Don't hesitate, write down exactly what you want or have dreamed of doing at some time but have yet to achieve. Take all the time you need. Please do this before proceeding with this chapter.

Once you've listed your dreams and desires, you'll have many of the aspects of your purpose and destiny in writing. I say "many" because you'll undoubtedly have included some dreams and desires that are yours but not necessarily inspired by God. These may not be outside the will of God, yet they may be items you just feel you'd like to do. It will be up to you to discover which are your own ideas and which are truly *His* will. Don't worry at this point which is which; you'll know without a shadow of a doubt before you finish reading this book. (I've written an entire chapter in this book to help you learn how to confirm what is and is not God's will for you.) Your desires are often in line with what you are made to be and to do anyway.

> "A passionate desire and an unwearied will
> can perform impossibilities."
> —*Sir John Simpson*

DO WHAT YOU LOVE

By writing down the desires you possess, you'll uncover many that are to be the focus of your destiny. You must believe that whatever desires God gives you will be *inside* His purpose for you, as a part of your destiny. Jesus didn't give His life only to keep you guessing about the life He has for you, and He won't take the chance of giving you a purpose and destiny so foreign to your own desires that you might say no to them!

Jesus gave away His life so that we, in turn, could give away our lives, doing His will in the manner best suited to our personalities and backgrounds. That doesn't mean you won't be sent to a foreign mission field or that you'll live in comfortable surroundings your entire life, although either may be true. It does mean, however, that if you are to live in luxury or if you are to go to the African bush, you'll be consumed with the desire to do so. God will give you the desires of your heart—first the desire, then the ability. If He wants you in Africa, you will *want* to go to Africa.

I've always loved performing. It's been my burning desire for my entire life. I love being in front of people entertaining, instructing, or ministering. I even fulfilled my lifelong wish to be a professional entertainer by entering professional circus after college. But a year later, I gave up the rights to my life and handed them to Jesus. I walked away from circus and vowed never to perform it again unless it was to His glory. It never occurred to me that He *wanted* me to do just that! Within a few months, the Lord was directing me to begin a circus that would proclaim Jesus as Lord. He was giving me back what I loved most. Actually, it was what He had designed me for all along!

For seventeen years, I did what I loved as a circus acrobat. For twelve of those years, I had the time of my life doing the two things I loved most—circus and ministry. The Lord entrusted me with an anointing to win souls, heal the sick, and help people break free from the strongholds of Satan. It was awesome! But eventually it ended. When my circus years were over, I was not upset or even remorseful—I was elated! Why? Because God then revealed to me the next step in my destiny—something else I would love—and it also involved helping people.

Next the Lord led me into prophetic ministry. By the time He told me to make the change, I was more than ready for it, because He had put the desire for it in my spirit. Within a few months after I'd stepped away from circus, I was introduced to a prophetically gifted and humble group of ministers in Kansas City, and was asked to join their staff. The Lord told me to serve these men, and I did so as a pastor, even though I felt I had neither the gifts nor the temperament for it. What I did have, though, was the desire to serve, which had also been placed in my heart by God. The prophetic gifts God had instructed me to pursue were nurtured during my tenure as a pastor with these ministers.

Since that time, I've gone through several more transitions in my destiny. I'll undoubtedly take a few more turns before I finish my course. I've come to understand that changes are not something to be feared but embraced. I'm totally confident that the Lord, my Father, will be sure to place the next desire in my heart when it's needed. I'm looking forward to future changes because I know I'll always be doing what I love, because I love Him and He loves me. It may take me some time to learn to love what He leads me into, but I know it will come.

Here's a question: Why aren't you doing what you love?

FOCUS

Focusing on what you do best will bring a surge of self-confidence. (It's rare that anyone else gives us a boost in this area, so why not do it yourself?) You'll probably be surprised at just how closely your gifts, skills, and desires match your personal purpose. Take your list of dreams and desires and highlight the items you are the most passionate about. What things, when you think about doing them, really get your heart racing? Mark the top five items in some way.

Next, take your list of gifts and skills list and place it next to your list of dreams and desires. Now, if you have it, take the "Focusing" worksheet from your *Life Planner* (or a separate sheet of clean paper) and place it on the table next to the other lists. Your paper should have the following headings on it: "Top Gifts," "Top

Skills," "Top Desires." Your assignment is to place your highest gifts, skills, and desires in the proper categories. By filling out this worksheet, you'll have a much clearer focus of what you're suited for.

What you are suited for will very likely be a part of your purpose and destiny. When I filled out my own focus list, I was struck by how the top five items in each category were so complementary to one another. I've since put each item on my list into practice.

MOTIVATOR OR HINDRANCE

Another aspect of desire is its ability to motivate us. A white-hot desire to accomplish, learn, and become someone specific supplies incredible power to get it done, as we saw in with basketball star Michael Jordan. God is not ignorant of this. He's established a covenant with His people based upon extraordinary and bountiful promises. Aren't heaven and the soon return of Christ desires in our hearts? Don't we long for freedom? Aren't we consumed with doing the will of God? Our desires can spur us on to amazing acts of achievement.

That's the power of desire! Desires and dreams in the heart of a believer are usually *not* evil. Most desires of dedicated Christians are inspired by God. But I've found that many believers are paralyzed in the pursuit of their dreams and desires because they fear that what they want to do is not in the will of God and that it may never happen. Others think it's somehow wrong to even have such dreams and desires. I believe that neither could be further from the truth!

"Whatever you like to do, just find a way to do it. The
biggest mistake people make in life is not trying to make
a living at doing what they most enjoy."
—*Malcolm Forbes*

TAKE NO SUBSTITUTES

My dear friend Chris, while in his early twenties, came to me with a dilemma. He was torn between what his heart desired and what he thought his parents wanted him to do. He longed to be a pastor, but he was sure his parents wanted him to be a dentist. They were talking about pre-med classes and then dentistry school, while all he could think about was pastoring. His problem stemmed from the fact that he so respected his parents' authority and wisdom that he felt his desires couldn't be right. He was motivated to do ministry, but he was hindered from pursuing that destiny through fear.

I encouraged Chris first to be totally honest with himself. He wanted to be a minister, and he admitted that he would be miserable as a dentist or anything else because of this truth. We then spoke with his parents, who were delighted at his desire to go into ministry! They had suggested dentistry simply to help him choose something, lest he choose nothing. Since his mother was in the dental field, both of his parents' were naturally inclined to suggest he go in that direction. Chris found that his fear was completely unwarranted. His paralysis vanished instantly! Chris has been in full-time pastoral work for many years now.

The bottom line of this story is that Chris had an inner, inescapable desire for ministry but thought that it had to be wrong because of his parents' leaning toward dentistry. In reality, the only wrong thing Chris could have done would have been to choose dentistry! Once Chris came to terms with what would really make his heart sing, there was no turning back. He knew it was the will of God, and the Lord confirmed it many times over.

FINAL THOUGHTS

The real lesson here is knowing with certainty that our dreams and desires are not going to get us in trouble with our Creator.

There is only one way to be sure that's true—ask Him. I realize that many people don't know how to do that or how to know He's given them an answer. I struggled with those questions for a few years myself. But then I discovered that the Lord had given us several ways to rid ourselves of any doubt. In the following chapters, I'll give you a foolproof system for confirming everything you feel God reveals to you. But first you need to know how the master principle of dreams and desires can become a source of life wealth.

6

WHAT'S MY LIFE ROI?

"You must invest before you can harvest."
—*Bill Greenman*

THE LAW OF RECIPROCITY

This brings us to the most important principle in this book, that of investing in others in order that you may receive what you need when you need it. In 2 Corinthians 9:6, we are told, *"Now this I say, he who sows sparingly shall also reap sparingly, and he who sows bountifully will reap bountifully."* Whatever we sow, or invest, we will reap, or receive a return on investment (ROI). My suggestion to you is that you invest bountifully, or sow the ministry of helps, into the lives of others who need assistance with their destinies. By so doing, you'll have a bountiful ROI to help you expand your own purpose and destiny. I call this principle "life wealth" because it can be found in any area of life into which you sow.

"This is the miracle—the more we give away to others, the more we have."
—*Anonymous*

The ministry or gift of helps is perhaps the most misunderstood ministry in the church today, yet it's also the most needed. A powerfully anointed ministry gift, helps is listed along with other well-known gifts as apostleship and prophecy. (See 1 Corinthians 12:28.)

Helps is not a gift to be taken lightly, but one that should be utilized by anyone who knows his or her life purpose. People with the gift of helps are to assist others with their purpose and destiny. We all need the ministry of helps. Actually, we all need to operate in this gift from time to time. Any purpose that God gives you will be too big for you to handle alone. "Lone Ranger" Christianity is not God's idea of quality ministry. He will create in you a need of others, and He will call upon you to be such a helper for others.

Let me give you an example from my own life. When the dream of Circus Alleluia first came into my heart, my wife Meg and I moved to Tampa, Florida, to begin. Once there, we began to attend a small independent church in the northeast section of town. I shared my vision with the pastor, Dale Brooks, and he immediately urged us to make it a part of his church. We took his advice. Almost immediately, we began to invest a major portion of our time and energy not into my circus dream but into Dale's dream for his church.

I knew how the law of reciprocity—giving and receiving—worked. Meg and I had employed this law to climb out of debt after quitting the professional circus world. I knew that it would work in any area of life where we needed help, so I determined to invest the majority of my time and energy into Dale's vision in order to reap a harvest when it was time for me to start my circus ministry.

I made myself available for whatever task was needed. At that time, there were approximately twenty-five people attending the church services on Sunday, so volunteer help was at a premium. Meg and I cleaned the bathrooms, vacuumed the carpets, scrubbed the outdoor baptistery, and mowed the acreage. We gave our time and labor, not for a few weeks, but for several years, even after we had begun the circus. We taught the youth group, ran the printing press, sang in the choir, and took cars to the repair shop. Whatever needed to be done, we did it gladly. We were investing for the harvest needed in our own lives and ministry.

Meg and I also looked for other major ministries into which we could invest our time and energies. Whenever a large convention came to town, I volunteered my services as an usher or counselor. I did this to invest excellent time and effort into these ministries. I gave high quality effort by giving them my best—the best of my abilities, the best of my time, and, of course, the best of my finances—because I wanted and needed the best to come back to me! And it did. It continues to because we have continued to invest, not just in minstries, but in the lives and visions of many others.

THE ANTS HAVE IT

There is an ancient proverb noting that an industrious little ant is something to observe and learn from. It tells of how these little folk work hard through the summer when there is plenty to ensure a sufficient food supply during the winter months. This illustrates our need to invest in others during times when our own need is minimal. When my circus dream began to increase, I knew that I could reap the necessary ROI because I'd invested well. After several years of having investing into my pastor's vision and the visions of others, I began to see a bountiful harvest returning to me!

Even today, decades later, I still stand amazed at the return that comes my way. The servant attitudes of others and their willingness to help with my purpose and destiny are wonderful. People have volunteered to work with us behind-the-scenes where no one sees them, just as we had done for Dale. Many times they've volunteered even without us asking them to help! I know that the reason we are being blessed by these selfless people is because of all the years we spent (and still spend) investing our time and efforts into others. You truly do get what you give.

"There is no more noble occupation in the world than to assist another human being—to help someone succeed."
—*Alan Loy McGinnis*

Whatever your vision or purpose may be, you should sow quality time into someone else's purpose as a minister of helps. In fact, I believe that the majority of readers have the gift of helps itself. Why? Because leaders are not the majority; assistants are. Neither role is better or more important; it's just that leaders are few in God's scheme of things. Therefore, it stands to reason that the majority of people are ministers of helps to assist leaders in their purposes and in the development of their destinies. If yours is the ministry of helps, what an exciting purpose God has given you!

FINAL THOUGHTS

Examples of the ministry of helps are scattered across the pages of the Old and New Testaments. Even Jesus Himself operated in the ministry of helps, such as when He fed five thousand and healed the multitudes. He helped and assisted people to meet their needs. In fact, I don't believe God will give anyone a vision or purpose that doesn't in some way involve the ministry of both giving and receiving help.

Remember, any vision from God will always do two things: first, it will glorify God; second, it will help people. Visions, purposes, and destinies of mere survival are not God's plan for His church. You need people operating in the ministry of helps to further your vision from God. Therefore, before your need becomes too great, reach out and sow your time and effort into someone else's vision as a minister of helps. When you need it, your ROI will be there.

"Success in life has nothing to do with what you gain in life or accomplish for yourself. It's what you do for others."
—*Danny Thomas*

7

WHAT LANGUAGE IS THAT?

"But seek first His kingdom and His righteousness, and all
these things will be added to you."
—Matthew 6:33

Seeking the kingdom of God is a command, not an option. The Lord has visions and plans for each of us, and they all are inside His kingdom. Anything outside of God's kingdom is inside Satan's kingdom, and, according to Colossians 1:13, we have been delivered from that kingdom of darkness. Our kingdom is the kingdom of light, and in it, we find our personal purpose.

As Christians, our actions help to destroy Satan's kingdom on a daily basis. We tear down his strongholds and undo his works by the power of God working through us, doing all that Jesus did and even greater. (See John 14:12.) Assuming that you agree that the vision and purpose ordained for you by God are within the confines of His kingdom, we will look at discovering its exact location. Once that location has been established, we can begin to look at how to practically live out that purpose in the natural world.

Jesus states in Luke 17:21, "*Nor will they say, 'Look, here it is!' or, 'There it is!' For behold, the kingdom of God is in your midst.*" The King James Version reads, "*The kingdom of God is within you.*" The kingdom of God is inside each person who calls Jesus, Lord. A king always lives within the borders of his kingdom. When a person receives Jesus Christ as his Lord, God's Holy Spirit immediately comes to live inside that person's spirit. Therefore, it's logical to assume that if Christ lives inside us, His kingdom must also be inside us. And if our purpose is found in His kingdom and His kingdom is inside us, then our purpose is inside us, as well! See Figure #2 below.

Figure #2

Your Purpose Is
in God's Kingdom

Your Purpose

Your Purpose Is inside
God's Kingdom and
God's Kingdom Is
inside YOU!

God's ordained purpose for your life (including the entire plan for its completion that He has set forth) is inside you this very moment! It's lodged in your spirit because that's where the

kingdom of God resides. Your purpose is a seed, and God's kingdom is its shell. But a purpose locked inside the kingdom of God
within you is worthless. Neither you, the unsaved world, nor followers of Christ will ever receive its benefits unless *you* release it.

> "Man's search for meaning is
> the primary motivation in his life."
> —*Viktor Frankl*

THE REVEALER

Your purpose lies within your spirit, but its plans and details
must be revealed to you. The Lord left us clear instructions as to
exactly who will do the revealing and how it will be revealed. Have
you ever called a business and explained to someone your need for
help with a specific problem? Perhaps you gave a representative all
the details only to hear that he or she couldn't help you and that
you needed to speak with someone else! My point is this: When
you want results, speak with the right person. When you want the
Lord to reveal your purpose to you, tune into the right Source.

We said in an earlier chapter that when we receive a personal
vision, a revealed word from God, it will restrain or guide us. The
Holy Spirit of God will reveal our purpose to us, which will lead
and guide us for the rest of our lives. It's the Holy Spirit's assignment here on earth to lead us in such a revelatory way:

> *But when He, the Spirit of truth, comes, He will guide you
> into all the truth; for He will not speak on His own initiative,
> but whatever He hears, He will speak; and He will disclose
> to you what is to come. He shall glorify Me, for He will take
> of Mine and will disclose it to you. All things that the Father
> has are Mine; therefore I said that He takes of Mine and will
> disclose it to you.*　　　　　　　　　　　　　(John 16:13–15)

Jesus states here that the Holy Spirit will reveal to us all that is the Father's. *"All"* means "all-inclusive." Such revealing must include our personal purpose and destiny! The Holy Spirit will reveal to us the plans that our Father in heaven has ordained for our lives. They will always be bigger than we can imagine and larger than we can carry out on our own. That's why we've been given the Revealer—and He has His own special language.

THE LANGUAGE OF THE HOLY SPIRIT

The Lord gave us a wonderful promise when He said, *"My sheep hear My voice, and I know them, and they follow Me"* (John 10:27). Jesus comforts us by stating that we, His sheep, do hear His voice. His declaration that we follow Him implies that we also understand Him when He speaks to us. But here lies the frustration of many believers—learning to hear and understand so that they can follow God accurately with the utmost confidence.

Most of us believe that we can hear the Lord's voice; we're just not sure which voice is His. Is it Jesus, us, the devil, or the pizza we ate last night? To help us learn one voice from another, the Lord has given us the Holy Spirit to revealer God's will. It is the Holy Spirit's job to speak to us in such a way that we can hear, understand, and follow. Our job is to learn how to listen.

In order to establish the ability to speak to us, the Holy Spirit created His own unique language, a language composed of thoughts, ideas, visions, and dreams. He plants these communications in us as seeds within the fertile soil of our spirits and minds. However, if we don't understand the language of the Holy Spirit, we won't clearly hear or be able to obey. Let me explain.

To become a successful circus performer, I was forced to learn a new and unique language known only in the circus world. Until I knew the names of the various pieces of rigging and the meaning of specific commands, I found it virtually impossible to contribute to the team or shows. As a beginner, I made many errors due to my ignorance of the language (some were quite painful!). When someone ordered me to "take a foot on that block and set a bite," I had no idea what to do. It was frustrating for everyone involved. Not only was I continually embarrassed by missed assignments, but my coaches and fellow performers were also often hindered. When I finally mastered the language, however, I became capable of understanding instructions and carrying them out.

The parallel to our individual purpose should be obvious. If we don't understand the language of the Holy Spirit, we roadblock both our own lives and the overall plan for the Lord's church. We have to learn the language of the Holy Spirit in order to live out our destinies as individuals, thereby advancing the master work of God's will.

God's Word contains over two hundred thirty instances in which the Lord spoke to His people through visions and dreams. These visions and dreams are detailed in thirty-two separate books of the Bible, with fourteen such occurrences in the book of Acts alone. In fact, the entire last book of the Bible, Revelation, is all one visionary experience given to the apostle John. The extraordinary language of the Holy Spirit was regularly used to communicate God's purpose and plan to both individuals and His people as a nation. Moses saw a burning bush and heard the audible voice of God explain his life's purpose. (See Exodus 3.) The apostle Paul saw a bright light and heard a voice proclaiming what his purpose was. (See Acts 9.)

I'm not speaking only of these types of visions or awesome angelic appearances. Neither am I saying that the Holy Spirit's language is limited to those dreams and visions experienced while you're asleep. The language of the Holy Spirit also includes God-inspired thoughts and ideas. The Holy Spirit will skillfully insert His words and thoughts into your mind. You may never hear an audible voice; most people never do. But daily, at any moment,

God can flash His ideas in your brain. Sixty-five thousand images flow through the average person's mind each day. Doesn't it make sense that God would be a part of at least some of those ideas and thoughts? Throughout His Word, God proves again and again that this is a major avenue of His guidance for His people.

Jesus was led in this way during His life on earth. He was guided by the Father on a moment-by-moment basis, for He proclaimed:

> *Truly, truly, I say to you, the Son can do nothing of Himself, unless it is something He sees the Father doing; for whatever the Father does, these things the Son also does in like manner. For the Father loves the Son, and shows Him all that He Himself is doing; and the father will shown Him greater works than these, so that you will marvel....I can do nothing on My own initiative. As I hear, I judge; and My judgment is just, because I do not seek My own will, but the will of Him who sent Me.* (John 5:19–20, 30)

Jesus was so in tune with the Father that He was able to receive exact instruction and never once missed an opportunity to see, hear, or do His Father's will. This instruction probably came through the thoughts and ideas He received during His times of prayer, rather than through supernatural visions or an audible voice. The New Testament records only one vision that Jesus experienced during His tenure on earth, which occured on the Mount of Transfiguration, when He was engulfed in the glory of God as He talked with Elijah and Moses. (I am not saying that God didn't give Jesus *other* visions, dreams, and so forth, but just that this is the only one recorded.)

The Bible records that the Father spoke audibly to Jesus two times during His human life; both were merely to confirm the fact of Christ's sonship—a fact Jesus was already well aware of. With this in mind, it is safe to assume that the Father spoke to Jesus through His thoughts—through His spirit—as a regular, daily means of communication.

For example, how did Jesus know it was time to be baptized by John? Or by what means of communication did the Holy Spirit lead Him into the desert to be tempted by the devil? I believe that it was through the thoughts and ideas flowing in His mind. Many times in Scripture we are told that Jesus departed to a lonely place to pray. (See, for example, Mark 1:35; Luke 5:16.) When He returned from the mountains or from the desert after those times of prayer, He would often perform miracles. Why? Because more of the purpose and plans for His life were revealed during His time with the Father.

In John 12:49, Jesus stated that He did not speak on His own initiative, but that His words were given to Him by God. How did those words come to Him? They came through His thoughts and ideas. The Holy Spirit will speak to us in like manner concerning the purpose and destiny He has for our lives, thus fulfilling Jesus' promise that we will do the works He did and greater.

Such guidance is more common than physical communication from the Father (i.e., an audible voice, sending an angel, and so forth). Our ability to discern God's still, small voice with clarity and confidence is the result of a solid relationship with Him. (See 1 Kings 19:9–12.) Such communication requires a deep, meaningful life of faith. Jesus obviously exemplified such faith for us to follow.

Merriam-Webster's 11th Collegiate Dictionary defines *vision* as "a picture that you see in your mind," so it's a mental sight. Many times the Holy Spirit will show you actual images of the things He wants you to do. (Look again at John 5:19–20 and notice that the word "show" is used twice in conjunction with Christ's submission to the Father's will, implying sight of some sort.) The Holy Spirit plants pictures within us as He communicates God's will to us— as well as our purpose.

I believe that the Father did this for Jesus on a daily basis. The Father gave Jesus mental sight of the complete picture of His will. Jesus then talked about the answers to the problem—the finished product—rather than the problem or the steps to completion. Be it healing a paralytic man or raising the dead, Jesus saw the answer. And since Jesus is our example, it's reasonable to believe that God will do the same for us.

LISTENING TO THE SPIRIT

Over the past several decades, I've grown accustomed to listening carefully to the amazing language of the Holy Spirit. When I pray, I'm surprised if He does not share with me a vision, a divine thought, or a mental image of some sort. As I intercede for someone or for a specific situation, I do so fully expecting the Holy Spirit to reveal to me precisely how I should pray for the need to be met, in His language. After all, He knows exactly what needs to be done and desires to work with His children, so I should well expect Him to give me the solution. That's not arrogance, it's the work of the kingdom. And it works!

For instance, I was once praying for a young woman who had come to me and pleaded, "I need direction in my life!" As I prayed for her, I saw a picture in my mind of her sitting in a large wing-backed chair, hunched over an old, dark-stained wooden desk. Sitting on the upper right-hand corner of the desk was a tiny delicate brass and milk-glass lamp. The woman was busily writing something in a large black three-ring notebook. There were several other notebooks cluttering the desk's well-worn surface. In the deep gray of the dimly lit room, I could see a silver-haired old woman wrapped in a large-knit shawl, sitting silently in an wooden rocking chair.

As the image disappeared, I realized that this was the Holy Spirit speaking to me about the direction He had for this woman's life. I shared the vision the Holy Spirit had given me with the young lady. I told her my interpretation: "Whatever you were writing in that notebook, whatever you were working on at that moment, and whoever that old woman was in the background, that's your direction."

Her eyes widened as she listened to me. Then, somewhat awe-struck, she told me that, just the night before, she had been at a relative's house working at the very desk I had described. She had been formulating plans to help her elderly grandmother, who was actually sitting in the room behind her while she was working. God had shown me, through the language of the Holy Spirit (thoughts, ideas, pictures, and visions), exactly what the woman had been doing the night before! Then the young woman acknowledged that she had always had a desire to help older people. I assured her that her desire was part of the Lord's direction for her life. The anxiety on her face suddenly lifted and was replaced by an expression of peace.

The Lord states again and again that He shows no partiality and will give us all what He has given to Christ. If Jesus knew the language of the Holy Spirit, then you and I can also. But we must develop this divine form of communication. It demands time spent in prayer and worship. It requires sacrifice. But the cost versus the benefit is definitely in our favor.

"Once a new idea springs into existence, it cannot be unthought. There is a sense of immortality in a new idea."
—*Edward de Bono*

FROM SEED TO FRUITION

Take a moment now and look around the room you're in. Every object you see began as a mere idea, an inspired thought in someone's image-filled mind. That thought or mental picture eventually became the physical reality you now experience. Now, that idea didn't just leap from the person's creative mind into reality. Instead, the idea had undergone many phases of development before it materialized. Likewise, your own purpose will be revealed and lived out in a step-by-step process. And this purpose is in you right this very second!

When the Father reveals to you His purpose for your life, it will begin as one simple yet powerful thought or idea. That thought or idea is like a seed, having within itself the entire plan of how that purpose, your destiny, will come about. In every acorn is the plan for a mighty oak tree. Each kernel of corn contains the potential to become a corn stalk with many ears of corn, holding thousands of new kernels. Likewise, the seed of your purpose conceived in the womb of your spirit and mind contains the complete plan for its achievement. Those detailed plans will continually be revealed to you in the same manner as the first thought or idea came to you—by the picturesque language of the Holy Spirit.

For me, it was the idea of becoming a professional performer of some sort. That thought was like a seed, having within itself the entire plan of how that purpose would come about. It took almost twenty years to get me to the place I could bear the right fruit from that seed, but it eventually happened.

"Imagination is the preview of life's coming attractions."
—*Larry Eisenberg*

TWO EXPERIMENTS

All this information is great, but if you can't apply it in a practical way, it's just ink on paper. I want you to personally know these truths. By performing the following experiments, you'll experience the truths we've just discussed. One will be geared toward quiet listening and the other toward specific thinking. I strongly suggest that you perform both many times. I believe that you'll gain valuable insight from each exercise every time you attempt it. Be sure to have a pen and paper handy.

EXPERIMENT #1

Take a moment right now, or at your earliest possible convenience, and ask the Lord to reveal His purpose for your life in thoughts, pictures, and ideas. Don't tell Him how to speak to you; only ask Him to let reveal to you what His will is for your life. Listen to the Holy Spirit's unique language, and, as you listen, be ready to write down whatever comes to your mind. Don't disregard any thoughts or pictures you may see in your imagination. Don't worry about whether or not you believe them—just write them down.

No one's going to hold you accountable for anything you receive. You're simply creating an opportunity for the Holy Spirit to speak to you. This is a faith exercise because you are expecting the Holy Spirit to be the prominent voice within you. Give Him the okay to dominate your thinking and imagination. Be prepared to listen quietly for at least ten minutes.

> "Be more impressed with ideas
> than you are with things or events!"
> —*Bill Greenman*

When you've received some thoughts, ideas, or images, and have written them down, look at them and ask yourself how they line up with what you really like to do. Remember, we're talking about purpose here, not the actual plans and steps to carry it out.

Then, without giving them a great deal of thought, jot down some answers to the questions below, which will help you to focus your thoughts.

+ Do the thoughts/ideas/images sound like you and your desires and dreams?

+ Would you enjoy doing these things for the rest of your life?

+ Are they in line with your gifts?

No one but you will be able to answer these questions. They're merely to get you thinking about the possibilities that your purpose might offer. Again, no one will hold you to anything you write down in these exercises, but it's likely that you'll get some important information from the Lord during this experiment.

"Master your imagination, and you will never be its slave."
—*Bill Greenman*

EXPERIMENT #2

Now use your sanctified imagination for a moment. Before you answer the questions below, ask the Holy Spirit to lead you through them, painting the answers upon the canvas of your imagination. Don't spend a great deal of time on any one question, but try to let the answers flow quickly from the Lord. Be ready to write as you go.

Picture yourself at the end of your life, having lived without any limitations, financial or otherwise. Now answer these questions:

+ What do you want your obituary to say?

+ What was your major focus of accomplishment?

+ What kind of person were you?

+ Who did you work with?

+ Where did you go?

+ Where did you live?

+ How did you affect the world?

+ Which of your accomplishments continue to produce results that help people and will continue to bring glory to God, even after your death?

+ How did you set your legacy in motion?

This second experiment is my favorite because it allows us to think on different things than we normally let ourselves consider. I'm sure that this experiment will either cause you to realize your limited ability to let God enlarge your thinking or captivate you with what you see. Either way, I hope that you took a major step forward in learning the language of the Holy Spirit, which is the main purpose of these experiments.

FINAL THOUGHTS

As we go through this book together, we'll build on these and other questions that are helpful to consider in achieving our life-long purpose. And, if you tried these experiments and came up "empty-minded," don't worry. Remember the general orders given to all believers that we discussed in a previous chapter. They can fill your life with purpose and destiny the rest of your days! Also, you'll receive some very specific information in the following chapters that will fill the void and bring you a lot of joy. And if you're wondering whether you actually heard from the Holy Spirit, rest easy. In the next chapter, I'll give you a foolproof system for confirming anything you feel the Lord has told you or shown you.

MASTER PRINCIPLE #2

PLAN YOUR FUTURE

"For this [reason] *I was appointed…in faith and truth."*
—1 Timothy 2:7

*"'For I know the plans that I have for you,' declares the
L*ORD*."*
—Jeremiah 29:11

I'm talking about planning every area of your life here, not just the financial or material aspects of your life, but also the spiritual, social, physical, mental, and emotional areas. I'm talking about being certain you have all the resources needed to accomplish what you were made to do. That will require understanding what those resources are, how to find them, and how to get them working for you. The main focus in this section is to give you the knowledge you need to acquire those resources. For more specific funding techniques in each area of life, see my other training materials found on my Web site. We will begin by learning how to confirm every word God gives you personally, so you can plan with certainty.

8

KNOW THAT YOU KNOW

"Every fact is to be confirmed by
the testimony of two or three witnesses."
—2 Corinthians 13:1

Once you begin to recognize the voice of the Holy Spirit, understand His language, and receive the purpose He has for your life, then you must be able to confirm, without a shadow of a doubt, that what you are receiving is actually from Him. Your enemy, the devil, will attempt to confuse and distract you. Friends and loved ones might not believe in your dreams. Even your own thoughts, imaginations, and ideas can rise up against you with doubts and fears. Therefore, to assist you in realizing your true purpose, the Lord has given us several ways in which we may confirm His leading.

Before listing any of these steps of confirmation, you should be building a solid, intimate relationship with your heavenly Father. Such a relationship requires time in prayer, Bible study, and fellowship with other committed Christians, as well as witnessing to those who've not heard about Christ. When you have a relationship with the Lord, it is much easier for Him to confirm His will to you, because you know His voice and the ways in which He works.

Let me illustrate. I have three children. When each was born, he or she was no more aware of me than of anyone else. They recognized neither my voice nor the touch of my hand. But as I spent time with them, they heard my voice, felt my touch, and saw my face again and again. Eventually, we established a relationship (at least as much as is possible with newborns). When I spoke or simply entered the nursery, my child would instantly respond to me, even if others entered the room with me. As my children grew and matured, they were able to express love through conversation and communication. The relationship I now have with my grown children was built upon the foundation of consistent, daily contact.

So it is with our heavenly Father. We have to take time to build that relationship. If we don't, the following steps of confirmation will be difficult to use. Only a truly committed believer will follow all the steps of confirmation, because performing them requires self-motivation and patience, and that's hard to sustain without the Lord's assistance.

> "Once you discover your God-ordained purpose,
> you must hold it under the bright,
> revealing flood lamp of His confirmation."
> —*Bill Greenman*

SEVEN STEPS TO REACH ABSOLUTE CONFIRMATION

You can use the following seven steps to confirm whether anything you desire is from the Lord. These steps are scripturally based and time-tested. You won't need to question your desires and dreams any longer; just put these seven steps into practice, and enjoy the freedom of being totally confident that the Lord has spoken to you. I know it sounds too good to be true, but we *are* dealing with the Creator of the universe here. He is an expert at letting His kids know His will beyond any and all doubt!

I've created a "Confirmation Checklist" for you, which is located in the *Purpose Master Planner*. If you don't yet have one, simply make your own checklist by placing these seven headings on a clean piece of paper. Then, as confirmations come to you, write them down under the appropriate heading.

STEP #1: PRAYER

> *When you pray, you are not to be like the hypocrites; for they love to stand and pray in the synagogues and on the street corners so that they may be seen by men. Truly I say to you, they have their reward in full. But you, when you pray, go into your inner room, close your door and pray to your Father who is in secret, and your Father who sees what is done in secret will reward you. And when you are praying, do not use mean-ingless repetition as the Gentiles do, for they suppose that they will be heard for their many words.*   (Matthew 6:5–7)

Jesus was laying the foundation for personal prayer. He explained that *when* we pray (not *if*), we should walk into our prayer room and shut the door behind us. We are to be alone with God, without the distractions of TV, phone, and other people. We should speak to the Lord in secret. If we do this, He promises to reward us outside the prayer room. One of the ways God rewards His kids is through a greater ability to hear His voice. My time in prayer is often my greatest time of inspiration. It was during those times prayer that I began to establish an unshakable relationship with Him and understand His language.

Through the thoughts, pictures, and words in your spirit and mind, along with feelings of assurance in your heart, God will communicate clearly with you. But you have to take time during your daily prayer sessions to listen for Him. We shouldn't be rude and monopolize the conversation; we need to sit quietly and let Him speak. He's our Father. If we truly love Him as we say we do, then we have to listen so that we can obey. Prayer must be a two-way channel if we're to receive clear confirmation.

STEP #2: INNER PEACE

> But the fruit of the Spirit is love, joy, peace, patience, kindness, goodness, faithfulness, gentleness, self-control.
>
> (Galatians 5:22–23)

Here we see that peace is a fruit the Holy Spirit will develop in our lives. If God is giving you a vision or dream that reveals His purpose for your life, He'll always confirm it with a feeling of peace within you. This is often referred to as the "witness" of the Holy Spirit. Here's a good way to test this issue of peace. When you think about your purpose—the vision set before you—when you dwell on it and daydream about it, do you have a peaceful feeling or an uneasy feeling? If your purpose is from the Lord, there will be peace and gentleness, without a hint of restlessness mixed in. (See Philippians 4:6–7.)

Also, by praying from a stance of faith, trust, and reliance upon God, you can know peace beyond the natural. By disregarding fear and anxiety due to your total trust in the Lord, you open the door to His presence and therefore His peace. This peace will set a supernatural guard over your thoughts, emotions, and beliefs of your heart, to keep out further fear and doubt.

Many times, I was plagued with fear and doubt about the things God had shown me concerning my purpose. But every time I deliberately trusted what the Lord had told me in prayer, fear and doubt lifted quickly. Then, in the face of circumstances that had not changed one bit, I had peace that all would be as He had said.

My wife used to scold me, saying that I never worried, so she had to worry for both of us. (I tried to tell her that worry is a sin, but my delivery must have been flawed, for it rarely produced the effect I'd hoped for. Is that a surprise?)

Now we will learn the "peace drills." The purpose of these drills is to give you firsthand experience with the feelings and thoughts that accompany the Lord's peace, as compared with the opposite. After you perform each drill, be still for a moment, checking to see if there is a feeling of peace within you. Then, write down your impressions of those feelings for later study.

Drill #1: Think about something you know, without a doubt, to be God's will, such as going to church or reading the Bible.

Drill #2: Think about something you know is absolutely *not* God's will, such as stealing or lying.

Then consider the following questions, which will help you evaluate your feelings:

+ What does God's peace (or the absence of it) feel like?

+ How is your physical state effected by this peace or the absence of it? For example, what happened to your muscles and facial expression?

+ What do you experience in your heart, your inner man?

+ Where do your thoughts take you during this time of peace or the absence of it?

I suggest that you perform this drill again and again until you have a strong understanding of God's peace—what it feels like and what if feels like without it. Get to know those feelings, for they'll be vital in helping you pursue God's will throughout your life. Remember this point when confirming your purpose (or whether anything is from the Lord): If there is no peace, don't move toward that idea or goal! At least not immediately, but more on that in a moment.

STEP #3: THE WORD OF GOD

Your word is a lamp to my feet and a light to my path.
(Psalm 119:105)

All Scripture is inspired by God and profitable for teaching, for reproof, for correction, for training in righteousness.
(2 Timothy 3:16)

These two verses explain that God's Word is both a light to assist in our search for direction, and a tool to train us in the areas needed to accomplish our goals. The Lord desires not only to light our path but also to equip us for the journey. His Word is more than able to handle both tasks. Please understand that the purpose God gives you will never contradict the Bible but will always be in line with it. Here are three methods God may use to confirm His will to you through His Word.

Method #1: Illumination

If you are reading the Bible one day and a verse seems to leap off the page at you, and it's in line with what you feel you've heard from the Lord, it may be a positive confirmation for you. A verse may seem to "stand up." You may find yourself reading it over and over again. This is one way God confirms His purpose, or a vision, thought, or idea, to you.

Method #2: Repetition

The exact same Bible verse pertaining to your purpose or something you're asking God about may come across your path several times in one day or over a short period of time. You may hear it spoken by a friend, read it in a book, hear it on the radio, or found it in the Bible itself during your daily reading. Many times, such repetition of the same Scripture is the Lord confirming to you that you've heard from Him.

Here's an example. Meg and I were living in Fort Collins, Colorado, when the Lord told me that we needed to move to Tampa, Florida, and begin Circus Alleluia Ministries. I had no doubt that I'd heard from the Lord, but I knew that Meg would have a hard time with it. I had dragged her around the country before—chasing my dreams of stardom—and I refused to do it again. So, I told Meg what I believed the Lord had said to me and assured her that we would not go unless He confirmed it to her, as well. She agreed to fast and pray with me for three days about the matter.

Partway through the first day, she came to me and said that she had her answer. Three times that morning, from three unrelated sources, the Lord had brought to her mind the Scripture concerning wives submitting to their husbands. She was convinced, and we moved soon after.

Method #3: References

Another way the Lord may use His Word to confirm a thought or idea is by dropping Scripture references into your mind through the Holy Spirit. Many times as I've prayed over something I felt was from God, several references to specific Bible books and verses would rapidly enter my mind. Whenever this happens, I write them down and immediately look them up. Sometimes, these verses confirm my idea, depending on whether or not God is the author of it. God can also give Scriptures to confirm that your idea or vision is *not* His will. One thing you can be sure of is that if a thought, idea, vision, or purpose is from the Lord, He will *always* confirm it by His Word.

STEP #4: WISE COUNSEL

The way of a fool is right in his own eyes, but a wise man is he who listens to counsel.   (Proverbs 12:15)

Through insolence comes nothing but strife, but wisdom is with those who receive counsel.   (Proverbs 13:10)

Many plans are in a man's heart, but the counsel of the LORD will stand.   (Proverbs 19:21)

Success is pretty much guaranteed when you enlist wise counsels. The focus word here is *"wise."* A wise counselor is someone who is already experienced in the area you're seeking information. If you need wise counsel in finances, you talk to someone with expertise in money matters. If you need wise counsel in cars, you approach someone experienced in that area. But if you go to the plumber when you need your car fixed, you may not receive the wisest counsel available.

But the wisest counsel of all is the counsel of the Lord. In the verses above, we see that only His counsel stands long-term. This said, it is always best to seek wise counsel from godly people who have the most experience in the specific area you're seeking counsel. So seek godly counsel from people who have experience in the same area of your purpose or vision.

It's mandatory to get wise counsel to confirm that what you receive is from the Lord. Yes, it's time-consuming, but it's worth it. Better to take the time now to be sure of yourself than to take the time later to correct yourself. Going slow, after all, is a great way to avoid problems.

Another benefit of seeking wise counsel is that others can "plus" your ideas and plans by adding something positive to them. I recently sat with a friend who had become a wise counselor to me in business matters. I shared with him my ideas for marketing some items. He took less than a minute to peruse the papers I handed him, then gave me several more things to do that proved extremely beneficial. Never underestimate the deep well of additional plans and ideas that a wise counselor can offer. They'll save you much time, heartache, and probably money.

STEP #5: CIRCUMSTANCES

The Lord can manipulate and control natural circumstances to confirm His Word to you. Through normal, daily happenings, the Lord can give you complete clarity concerning His direction for you. Many Christians often refer to the cliché "The Lord seemed to open the door" when referring to this type of guidance. This *is* a biblically based thought, yet it can be a dangerous one if taken as the only means of confirmation.

The reference to "opened" and "closed" doors comes from the apostle Paul's mention of it in 1 Corinthians 16:8–9: *"But I will remain in Ephesus until Pentecost; for a wide door for effective service has opened to me, and there are many adversaries."* Obviously certain circumstances indicated that evangelism was in season in Ephesus, and Paul meant to harvest some souls. But to think that Paul was acting only on circumstantial evidence would be wrong. At that point in Paul's life, he had many years of missionary work under his belt and was well versed in the guidance of God's Spirit. In fact, in this same letter, Paul teaches on the supernatural gifts of the God and the master plan He has for the church—each member being specifically placed within His body. Paul did not base his actions on open doors alone, and neither should we.

Let me share a personal example with you. My wife, Meg, and I were seeking confirmation whether or not to buy a certain house. During our time of seeking, several circumstances fell into place that all pointed toward a direct confirmation of the word we felt God was giving us to buy the house. One such circumstance was that the owner of the house we were renting wanted to move back into the house on a certain date. That date was directly in line with the time that we could move into the house we desired to purchase. Another circumstance that fell into place was the amount the seller required as a down payment for the house. It was almost the exact amount we had just received from an inheritance. We eventually bought the house.

Pinball Problems

These circumstances, although quite convincing, were not the deciding factor in our purchase of that house. We considered these only as part of the confirmation we sought. Circumstances should never be employed as the only means of direction or confirmation. By applying circumstances as your sole means of confirming a word from the Lord, you may find yourself bouncing like a pinball from circumstance to circumstance, without ever really reaching the goal the Father has set before you. A pinball is directed by whatever it bumps into. Led and guided completely by its circumstances, it actually has no direction at all and accomplishes nothing of lasting value. In order to avoid the pinball trap, you must trust circumstances *only* if they're in line with the other points of confirmation discussed here.

STEP #6: SUPERNATURAL HAPPENINGS

God uses the supernatural because He is supernatural. He uses open visions and dreams. He appears to people or has His angels appear to them. God can speak in an audible voice from the clouds or from a burning bush. He can speak through prophecies, animals, and storms. Our Lord can cause oceans to part and trees to wither. He is a supernatural Being. That understood, let's look at His gift of prophecy, as it is given a lot of weight in confirming God's direction in many Christians' lives.

As an assistant pastor and elder in two churches, each of several thousand members, and as a traveling minister, I've been both thrilled by the use and shocked by the abuse of the gift of prophecy. Many wonderful words of direction have been given by God through anointed saints, and much good has been done. I have marveled at this gift in young and old alike. But I've also sat heartbroken in many counseling sessions as I listened to the stories of those who had been devastated by "personal" prophecies. They had followed the prophecy down to the letter, only to be blown out of the water by an enemy torpedo in the spirit when it did not manifest as promised. By receiving a "word" from a well-meaning brother or sister, they had run headlong into the snare of the devil. Never live out a prophecy without first confirming it through the guidance and confirmation of a spiritually mature, wise counselor and one or more of the seven steps of confirmation.

First Corinthians 14:29 admonishes us to judge prophecies. Receiving a prophecy without confirmation can lead to disaster, but a prophecy tested and approved by godly leadership can prove very prosperous. Also be alert to the spiritual maturity of the one prophesying. Although any believer can be used of the Lord to share a word of prophecy, it's wise to consider the source. Seek godly confirmation for every supernatural utterance to avoid costly missteps.

Again and again throughout the Bible, God uses supernatural happenings to lead, guide, and confirm His word and will to His people. However, I caution you again: Don't use the supernatural as the sole means of confirming that your purpose and ideas are from God. First, the Bible states that Satan himself can appear as an *"angel of light"* (2 Corinthians 11:14). Many brethren have been deceived in this way. Second, we must be cautious because supernatural events throughout biblical history were rare. Though we are seeing a dramatic increase of supernatural events as the time of Christ's return draws closer, we must always make sure that supernatural manifestations are not our only means of confirming the word we feel God has spoken to us.

STEP #7: TIMING

> *There is an appointed time for everything. And there is a time for every event under heaven.*   (Ecclesiastes 3:1)

If ever there was a stumbling block, this is it. I mean, you get a vision from God, and He confirms it. You know that you know that you know that you *know* it's right! Nothing on this planet (or off it) could convince you otherwise! So, you presume that right now is the time for it all to take place. It just makes sense, doesn't it? Wrong!

When the six steps of confirmation listed above are in agreement, you can be sure that God has spoken to you to confirm the word He has revealed to your heart. But if you launch out before His perfect time, you can still fail miserably. (Ask me how I know!) You must see to it that, when you confirm your purpose, you continue to seek God concerning the correct moment, the specific timing, to act on that purpose.

Remember, it's the Holy Spirit's job to lead you and guide you into all truth. All truth includes God's perfect timing. He'll reveal it to you, and it will come through His language of visions, dreams, thoughts, and ideas. For many, including myself, this is the most difficult step of confirmation, as it involves waiting for the Lord to reveal His timing. Our zeal often overpowers our patience. Too many plans have fallen short of God's intended mark by either being rushed or expired. God has a perfect time for your purpose and destiny. Find it and follow it.

Let me illustrate the importance of this seventh step. When my wife and I bought the house I mentioned earlier, it still needed a lot of work to be completely ready for our move in. But we had to move in anyway, and the pressure to complete the work created a great deal of friction between me and my wife. It seemed as though we would never get it all done. My wife began to ask questions, such as "Do you think we heard from God on this house?" and "Should we have done this?" Honest wondering can kill your faith…and your relationships.

We purposely thought back through our steps of confirmation and discussed each point. The confirmation for buying that home seemed crystal clear…until we got to the timing of our decision. We suddenly realized that we had never sought the Lord about *when* we should make the purchase. Over the next few days, as we sought Him on this point, He revealed that we (correction, I) had been premature. God had wanted us to pledge a portion of our inheritance money to church-related work. But we had known that we wouldn't have had enough money for our down payment on the house if we had first given to the Lord's work. We believe that if we had waited on God's timing, for Him to bring in the rest of the money we needed for the down payment, the owner of the house would have been able to complete the renovations, and we would never have experienced the anxiety of having to do the work ourselves.

It was a costly error, to be sure—both financially and relationally. We endured not only the pressure of finishing our home but also the distress of not paying off our commitment to the church project on time. This was not the ideal method of learning the lesson of God's timing, but it was a lesson that we'll never forget and hopefully will never repeat!

> "A confirmed word from God is settled forever
> in the heart of the receiver."
> —*Bill Greenman*

The seven steps of confirmation we've discussed here can deliver amazing peace in the midst of the storms that can rage within your mind. Knowing without a shadow of a doubt that the Lord has spoken His will to you brings boldness birthed from confidence. Please learn from the successes and failures I've mentioned here, and diligently use these steps of confirmation in all you want to do for both God and others.

FLEECES AND LOTS

I want to share two more confirmation steps with you concerning the purpose God puts in your heart. These are "putting out a fleece" and "drawing lots." I mention these with great caution, because while both are biblical and often effective, they can be extremely dangerous if used without the other steps of confirmation.

In Judges 6:36–40, we read about Gideon using a fleece—a sheepskin—to confirm a certain vision he'd received. To make sure that the Lord had spoken to him, Gideon laid a fleece on the ground one night and asked God to make the dew settle only on the fleece and not on the ground around it. The Lord did as Gideon had requested. The next night, Gideon tested the Lord again, asking Him to have the dew rest only on the ground, leaving the fleece completely dry. God did so. Gideon took these supernatural occurrences as a sign that he had received orders from the Lord, and, acting upon that confirmation, he led Israel to victory in battle.

Drawing lots is a method by which the apostles used to choose an apostle to replace Judas Iscariot. The use of this method was probably based on Proverbs 16:33, which states, *"The lot is cast into the lap, but its every decision is from the Lord."* The apostles prayed and asked the Lord to direct the drawing of the lots. When the lots were drawn, Matthias was chosen. (See Acts 1:21–25.)

As I mentioned, both these steps of confirmation are biblically based and effective. Both can be dangerous, however, because they deal with supernatural happenings. By employing these types of confirmations, you are *asking* the Lord to supernaturally intervene in your circumstances. This is an inferior form of guidance. You must remember that Satan can also manipulate natural circumstances.

As we study Gideon in Judges chapter 6, we see that he had a *weak* relationship with God. In verse 13, he questioned whether God had His hand on Israel at all, let alone on him. This explains why the Lord honored his requests. Because there was little communication taking place between Gideon and the Lord, God had few other options open to Him. Because Gideon is not a model of stong faith in the Lord, we should *not* be following or teaching his example as a sole means of confirming direction from God.

I don't ask my wife every morning to give me a sign that she is still my wife or that she will have supper ready when I come home from work. I know my wife. We communicate. We do not rely on signs and wonders to confirm our trust in each other because we have developed our relationship beyond that point. When we first began dating, we used romantic items and events to express to each other the love we had. Even though we still do so, such acts are no longer necessary in convincing each other of our feelings. Our relationship with the Father should be just as solid, if not better!

In the book of Acts, we also see the real reason the apostles picked the new apostle by drawing straws. They'd been trained by Jesus, who was no longer with them, and they had not yet established a spiritual relationship with the Holy Spirit as their Guide. Therefore, they were forced to use the only other means of confirmation they knew. They required a natural way—casting lots, as taught in the Old Testment, the only written Word of God available to them—by which to confirm the Word of God.

Years later, the story was quite different. The disciples had learned the art of being guided by the Holy Spirit through thoughts, ideas, visions, and prophecies. They *expected* the Lord to speak to them in those ways. When Paul and Barnabas were called out by the Holy Spirit—probably through a prophecy—during a gathering of prophets and teachers in Acts 13, there's no mention of casting lots. Instead, the word of the Lord came through men yielded to His Spirit. Their relationship with the Lord had grown to the point that they could hear Him from within. Even after they'd received the word of the Lord, they took more time to pray about it to be sure that it was confirmed to all. Only then were the two missionaries sent out to do the work of the Lord.

I caution you (and all puns are intended): Don't "get fleeced" or end up with the short end of the stick by using uncertain guidance systems. Never use these methods as your sole means of confirmation. Grow in your relationship with the Lord to the extent that you don't need such natural means, but instead you can trust the conviction and guidance of the Holy Spirit within you.

FINAL THOUGHTS

We have a Father who loves us beyond measure. He has a definite purpose and plan for each of our lives. To make sure that we discover His purpose and achieve His plan, He created the steps of confirmation that we've discussed in this chapter. We have to employ these steps in our daily lives, not only to know the overall purpose of our life, but also to confirm any instruction we feel the Holy Spirit is sharing with us. And once we've confirmed the will of God, we then have to take the next step of clarifying it for all to see.

9

SETTING YOUR ROOTS

"Write the vision; make it plain on tablets, so he may run who reads it."
—Habakkuk 2:2 (ESV)

WRITE IT DOWN

Prophet Habakkuk's command is a powerful one. God meant it for our long-term good and for the achievement of His dreams. The Lord knows that the written word is what solidifies the thoughts, ideas, and dreams in our hearts. It's the written word that touches the lives of those who read it. It's almost supernatural the way writing down an idea can transfer it from the invisible into the visible reality of this world. When we write down what we believe, what we desire to do; it starts moving us *toward* that desire and belief. It energizes us when we read it. God knew that would be the case. He wrote down His vision for His people and He commands us to do the same.

When you have a dream, vision, or purpose in your heart, forces will be released to stop it. Part of that opposition comes from your own insecurities, while the other part of that opposition comes from the forces of darkness that use your human frailties, and those of others, against you. Make no mistake, the devil and his demons are very real. If you're a Christian, Satan is your sworn enemy for life. Whatever he can take from you, he will, including your purpose. He'll cloud your mind with doubt, saying to you as he said to Eve in the garden, "Did God say…?" He'll contradict the word of the Lord, twisting its meaning and weakening its impact. His main goal is to get you to wonder about what you heard. If you start to wonder, you'll waver. If you waver, you won't act. And if you don't act, Satan wins by default!

Why is there a Lamb's Book of Life? Why were there scribes in Israel whose sole occupation was to copy the Scriptures so perfectly that not one dot or letter would be left out? Is God forgetful? Does He need to read these things every once in a while to stay focused or to keep up to speed with the times? Of course not! Writing down the Word of God, as well as God's personal word to us, is for *our* benefit. We are forgetful, just as Eve was. She had part of it right, but the smallest error cost her everything! God wants us to avoid as much speculation and poor memory as possible. Therefore, He instructs us to write down our visions, dreams, and purpose in a way that they are not only easy for *us* to remember pursue but also for those He sends to help us.

No believer is alone in his pursuit of his visions, dreams, and purpose. Our purpose in this life will meet the needs of and require the assistance of other believers. We need to share our dreams and let others be part of them. To do that, we must be sure that others know what those dreams are, hence Habakkuk's command. Later in this chapter, I'll discuss how to create what I call a "Destiny Overview" to begin the writing process for others to run with. But first I want to share the three personal reasons why you should write down your purpose.

1. It will help solidify that your purpose is from the Lord.

2. It will help you focus the details of that purpose.

3. It will cause you to commit yourself to the purpose.

With a written plan before you, the Lord can sink it deep into your soul.

LOOK FOR THE RUNNERS

Through Habakkuk, the Lord instructs us to inscribe our vision on tablets of stone. A message hammered into stone is permanent. A written vision can easily be stamped in our hearts. Habakkuk speaks of others who will read our written vision and then run with us to get it done. These verses imply that the runners should be able to read it quickly and easily understand it.

Participants in a race have to know the course they are supposed to follow in advance. Without a course map, they wouldn't know where to start the race, where to finish it, or which route to take in between. If the race director simply said to the runners, "This race will go from Los Angeles to New York City and back," their first question would be, "What route do you want us to take?" He might describe the route in full detail; but after a few miles, the runners will likely forget the details. The person who envisions the race must also envision the plan, or course for the race, and put it on paper for the racers. Without the plan, or the written directions, the runners may never finish the race at all!

Your purpose in this life is similar. The Lord has believers who will desire to assist you in accomplishing your dream. If there's no written course, direction, or plan for them to observe, then it'll be difficult for them to run with your purpose, no matter how enthusiastically you present it. You *must* write down your purpose. Multitudes of people are anxiously waiting for a dream—any dream—to run with! Although God's given His people personal visions of their purpose and destiny, only those who've written them down can expect to enjoy the rewards that come as others run with them.

BE THE RIGHT FIRE TRUCK

As I meditated on Habakkuk 2:2, the Holy Spirit spoke to me in His language. I saw a vision, a picture in my mind. In the picture, I saw a bright-red fire truck adorned with chrome handles and huge aluminum ladders sitting motionless by the curbside of a busy city street. There were no firemen around it. People walked by the truck and casually glanced at it, but no one stopped or seemed very interested in it.

Then I saw a second fire truck, which was an exact duplicate of the one sitting by the curb. But this truck came racing down the street with lights flashing, horn blowing, sirens blaring, and firemen hanging on the sides! It was heart-stopping! Everyone on the sidewalks turned their heads to see what was going on. Then an amazing thing happened. The very people who were all but ignoring the other fire truck started leaping into their cars and chasing the speeding truck to its destination! The Lord spoke to me in my spirit and said through my thoughts, "People don't follow parked fire trucks. They follow the truck that makes noise and is obviously heading somewhere important. When you write down your purpose and begin to proclaim it with conviction, that it will be done, people will follow you, too." That word changed my life. I put it into practice and found it to be true. I hope it changes yours in the same manner.

PEOPLE WHO NEED PEOPLE

When I launched Circus Alleluia Ministries, all I had to go on was one goal: Start a circus that gives glory to Jesus Christ. That was my total vision. It was not my purpose, although I thought so at the time. If I had allowed that vision to remain just an idea,

Circus Alleluia would never have become a reality, hundreds of thousands of people may never have heard the gospel of Christ, and tens of thousands of people would not have been saved, healed, or delivered from darkness. But I wrote down that thought. Actually, I began to write down every idea that could enlarge and advance that thought. Then I began to share those ideas with others.

An entire year passed before the first runner joined me in the race. That runner was my wife, and she did not come quietly! It took a wounded cat and the world's shortest three-day fast to convince her that I was not insane and that God was leading me. Soon after Meg joined me, my mother caught the vision. She was followed a few months later by my pastor, Dale Brooks. About three months after Dale began to run with us, the majority of his congregation jumped on board. Over the eleven years of its existence, literally thousands of people from across the U.S. and Canada came to believe in our vision and ran alongside us. Why? Because we didn't let the fire engine sit quietly by the curb! We hit the sirens, flashed the lights, and took off! We produced! We worked really hard! We did what we said we were going to do.

You must do the same thing with your purpose and destiny. People will run with you when you write down what you're going to do and then begin to do it. If you haven't yet written down anything about your purpose, take out a pen and paper and jot down just the main points of what you think it may be right now. That small vision can then be built into a vision statement, which you'll modify and work from for the remainder of your life. As you write down those simple things in your "Destiny Overview," I guarantee you that runners will read it and run with you.

LIKE A TREE

He is like a tree planted by streams of water…its leaf does not wither. (Psalm 1–3)

After several decades of study, I've concluded that there are six specific foundational roots we must establish within our hearts to find and articulate every purpose. They will draw the details from the river of God's Spirit. They are the headings in the "Destiny Overview" found in your *Purpose Master Planner*. If you don't have a *Purpose Master Planner*, take a sheet of paper and write them down as we discuss them here. Just be sure to leave yourself room under each heading to fill in the related information. If, after finishing, one or more of the stones are not filled in, you'll have an uneven platform upon which to build the rest of your plan.

ROOT #1: WHY?

Why do you have this purpose? Why do you want to see it done? Why will you refuse to quit along the way? Be careful not to answer these questions too quickly. Pat answers have little power and will not withstand the objections and roadblocks you'll encounter along the way. You need an unshakable confidence in your "why." It must be immovable, unstoppable, and irresistible! I can't give you the details of why you have the purpose you have or why you'll pursue it, but I can tell you that answering these questions is the most important stone of all. It's the cornerstone.

When you have an unshakable "why" engraved in your spirit, others will be drawn to it because so few people ever attain that level of *passion* for anything. Fearless explorers, great inventors, champion athletes, and courageous missionaries all know their why. They've experienced the help given by those who wish to see them fulfill it! *You* can know the same rewards, and you can help others reap their rewards just by inspiring them with your why. You'll be a light to those lost in the darkness of not knowing their own purpose. You'll take them with you. Know your why; then write it plainly for all to know and understand, as well.

ROOT #2: WHO?

> "Try not to become a man of success,
> but rather try to become a man of value."
> —*Albert Einstein*

Who are you? This is a question each person must answer for himself and for those running with him. Few of us take the time to think about it, but knowing who we are is paramount to knowing our purpose. Knowing who you are helps you to know whether you presently have the ability to accomplish the purpose before you. I know that sounds somewhat strange, so let me help you understand what I mean.

This "who" question must be answered in three distinct ways.

Personality

First, what's your personality like? There are several types of personalities, but we rarely know what ours is all about. Fortunately, there are now many questionnaires you can take—several that are free—that will show you with great accuracy which personality one you possess. Knowing your personality type—how you act, react, communicate, and interact with others—will make living out your destiny much easier. Certain purposes require certain personalities.

Experience

Second, you must know who you are as the sum of your experiences. What was your family like—especially your parents and, most importantly, your father? What have you accomplished to date? What have you learned? How have you been formed into the person you are by all of the above? How does your personal history affect *your* purpose? This may show you what parts of you line up with the kingdom of God and what you need to change about yourself to stay in line with the kingdom of God.

Philosophy

Third, you need to know your philosophy. (This is not a part of your Destiny Overview but is vital for you to know.) This includes your values, which are shaped by the factors above—your personality and experience—and which mold your character, whether good or bad. What do you believe? What do you stand for? What's the code by which you live and will carry out your purpose? Your philosophy, your code of ethics, will color everything you think, say, and do—including the sum of your purpose and destiny.

Because I believe that our personal philosophy is the most important of the three "who's" and second only to your "why" of purpose, I will spend the most time on it here. Furthermore, your personality and experience can be part of your personal study, as there's a multitude of books and courses to help you discover and understand them.

Our philosophy is the code we live by. It's what our personality and character are built on. For a Christian, that philosphy is clearly stated in Holy Scripture. Jesus said that if we love the Lord with all our heart, mind, and strength, and our neighbors as ourselves, we'll fulfill all the commandments. (See Matthew 22:37–39.) I've thought about those commandments for many years, and one day I came up with a simple way to remember them. I call it the "HIS Way" code.

H = Humility

Humility is not often taught as a character trait, but it should be. Most people think of humiliation when they think of humility. They equate "doormat behavior" (bowing to everyone else's will, letting yourself be used and abused) with humbling themselves. Nothing could be further from the truth. Jesus was the humblest man who ever walked the earth, but no serious student of His life would consider Him to be a doormat. It was His humility that caused Him to say that He was the Bread of Life and the Light of the World. He called Himself a Prophet and equated Himself with God. To understand the humility Jesus exemplified, we need read the epistle to the Philippians. Here is what the Word of God has to say about the subject.

> *Do nothing from selfishness or empty conceit, but with humility of mind regard one another as more important than yourselves; do not merely look out for your own personal interests, but also for the interests of others. Have this attitude in yourselves which was also in Christ Jesus, who, although He existed in the form of God, did not regard equality with God a thing to be grasped, but emptied Himself, taking the form of a bondservant, and being made in the likeness of men. Being found in appearance as a man, He humbled Himself by becoming obedient to the point of death, even death on a cross.*

(Philippians 2:3–8)

As we can see, humility is about giving your life for others, not letting them simply take advantage of you. It's about looking at others' lives and actually living, with sincerity, as though their needs are more important than your own. Christ's humility led Him to see His deity as nothing to strive for, but as something to give up for the salvation of others, even though it demanded a horrific death. That's powerful! That's humility.

To live a life of humility requires deciding to go against the grain of your pride and usually of society's view of you. But think of the rewards Jesus received. He not only got His life back in a glorified way, but His name became the greatest name in the universe—and He opened the way for millions, and perhaps billions, of people to follow Him into heaven for eternity! We'll never surpass Jesus' work on the cross, but we can enjoy His rewards.

The law that governs the universe, sowing and reaping, is applicable in the life of humility. God does not forget. The law that states it's more blessed to give than to receive also applies to the humble person. (See Acts 20:35.) How? Because when you genuinely give your life for others, to see their joy, it's better than any material reward could ever be! Why not ask the Lord to teach you about real humility and the tremendous rewards it brings? Giving your life away to lift others up is the best investment you can make.

I = Integrity

He who walks in integrity walks securely.   (Proverbs 10:9)

Better is a poor man who walks in his integrity than he who is perverse in speech and is a fool.   (Proverbs 19:1)

A righteous man who walks in his integrity—how blessed are his sons after him.   (Proverbs 20:7)

Vindicate me, O Lord, for I have walked in my integrity, and I have trusted in the Lord without wavering.   (Psalm 26:1)

O Lord, who may abide in Your tent? Who may dwell on Your holy hill? He who walks with integrity, and works righteousness, and speaks truth in his heart. He does not slander with his tongue, nor does evil to his neighbor, nor takes up a reproach against his friend; in whose eyes a reprobate is despised, but who honors those who fear the Lord; he swears to his own hurt and does not change; he does not put out his money at interest, nor does he take a bribe against the innocent. He who does these things will never be shaken.

(Psalm 15)

Integrity is such a powerful force. As you can see by these verses, integrity involves much of the Christian life. It's the way we walk out our life. It has to do with honesty, kindness, and keeping our word. More than a one-time event, integrity is to be our lifestyle. It affects not only us but those around us, especially our children. Furthermore, it allows us to boldly ask for vindication when we're in trouble.

Psalm 15 tells us that a man of integrity *never* stumbles. Do you understand what the word *never* means? It means not ever! Never stumble? I could enjoy that kind of life; couldn't you? Are you enjoying that kind of life right now? I want my integrity to be evident in my life every day, in every situation. That requires work on my part. Integrity is a decision, not a gift. God doesn't *give* you integrity; you develop it, cultivate it, seek it out, and form it in yourself with His help.

As a child, I became a pathological liar. It was sort of like a disease within me. I didn't even think about telling the truth if I thought a lie would do me better. This lasted long into my college years, and I didn't address it fully until I was in ministry. Yes, I stopped most of my lying by then—I was honest about almost everything—but still, if I was telling a story and thought a good embellishment would get a better laugh or more sympathy, I added a lie. Sad, isn't it?

After a session of storytelling one night with friends, Meg confronted me as to why I felt I had to lie about some things. I denied lying, of course, and a heated argument ensued. After the smoke cleared, the Lord convicted me, and I apologized and asked for her help. We decided that if she ever caught me lying, she had the right to stop me mid-sentence and correct me. Sounds simple to the ladies reading this; but I can just see the men curling their toes in their shoes! Let your wife correct you in public—are you nuts? No, I was desperate! I was desperate to be clean before God and my wife. I will tell you that it was unpleasant and embarrassing at times, and I lashed out at Meg more than once (then apologized later). But I can also tell you that together we were able to kill that unclean habit.

Psalm 15 emphatically states that a righteous man will keep his word, even if it does him harm. That's powerful in a world where signed contracts are not worth the paper they're written on. Will our excuses stand up before the presence of God and be counted worthy?

Take this little test to see what your "integrity quotient" is.

1. Do you embellish stories for effect?

2. Do you do anything in private that you would not do if your spouse or Jesus were present?

3. Is your word all that anyone ever needs in an agreement or commitment with you?

4. Do you give false or lame excuses to cover yourself when you don't keep your word?

5. Do your family members and friends feel confident that you'll keep your promises?

If you're to be a person whose philosophy is the guiding force of his existence, then your philosophy must be based upon the same integrity that Jesus walked in. It must be stumble-proof. You will gain so much more from nurturing integrity than you will if you neglect it.

S = Servant

Becoming a servant allows you to be in control of every situation—in the right kind of way. Think about the most giving servants you know. Do they seem to enjoy what they do for you? It's almost impossible for people with the gift of serving not to serve people. Again, my wife is my greatest example in this area. After a meal at someone else's home, she will always—unless told not to by the host—begin to clear the table and usually wash the dishes!

She is simply a great example of a person whose heart is totally given to serving others.

I didn't use to have this kind of heart. Mine was content to *be* served. But, of course, that's one reason the Lord arranged that Meg be my wife. I needed to change, and she was the change agent. When the Lord showed those verses in Philippians to me—that Jesus became as a bond-servant, a willing *slave* to the people around Him—I asked Him to give me that kind of heart, too. And He gave it to me.

I began to study serving and servanthood in the Bible. Jesus continuously taught His twelve disciples that to be the one in charge, you must serve. Being the "head honcho" was not the issue; being the willing servant was. I began to follow my wife's lead. I began clearing plates at every meal and offering help all over our neighborhood. One summer, I became the moving company for some dozen or so families in our church congregation who were moving to new homes because I had a truck and trailer. Many times, I was loading furniture late into the night to get them on their way. I took every opportunity to serve others. It didn't take long for my heart to relish this kind of life. It is, after all, the life of Jesus.

As our ministry grew, I began to teach our members to take on this servant's attitude. When we were on a tour with the circus, we stayed with the families of our sponsoring churches. I instructed our troupe to wash their host's dishes, clean their house, and help in any way possible. It became a great blessing to us all. We also were showered with heartfelt thank yous.

Your philosophy, whatever it may be, is what will reflect throughout your life. Be sure to stand every goal and dream of your destiny next to your philosophy to see if they complement each other. If they don't, change the inappropriate one. No philosophy or purpose will last long together when they're in disharmony. The only way to ensure harmony is to make sure that your philosophy and purpose are both God's.

ROOT #3: WHAT?

What will you do? What are the main goals of your mission? What do you plan to accomplish? The "whats" of your purpose, the main goals, will create the nuts and bolts that you will build with. In the next chapter, we'll take an extensive look at goals and goal-setting.

My purpose as a minister is to pray, make disciples, teach the Bible, evangelize, counsel believers, and support other leaders. My purpose is also to accomplish international projects in these areas. But I'm also called to be a businessman, and I have to know the things that God desires for me to accomplish in that realm. Because I know what my purpose is, I can then move onto making it happen—the "how" of my purpose.

ROOT #4: HOW?

This has to do with your specific methods of achieving your purpose. It's the details in a summarized or outlined form. When you work on your own Destiny Overview, you'll need to get detailed in the "how" of things. That means that you must understand your main and minor goals, and create appropriate objectives—the applicable, workable timeframes and quantitative outcomes of your goals, as well as how you'll accomplish them. This is your "working plan." Simply write down how you plan to accomplish your "whats."

For instance, Circus Alleluia was my evangelism vehicle during the 1970s and 80s. I had to write down objectives, such as how much equipment to buy, how many performers to gather, and how shows and ministry would blend. I had to discover how to make each of these happen. This is how one carries out goals.

ROOT #5: WHEN?

Time lines are mandatory for every part of your destiny. Time lines give you definitive points such as the beginning or ending. If you never set a time to begin or have an idea of when you want to end, you can't honestly judge your progress. A builder who takes two years to complete one house will not be in business very long. Time frames are a must.

You must have clearly defined time lines for every goal. You must have a definite date by which you will accomplish the many aspects of your purpose. Even though your purpose and destiny may expand as you discover new goals to achieve along the way, you should still set target dates and deadlines for each of the steps.

ROOT #6: WHERE?

Just where exactly will you live out your purpose? This can be tricky if your destiny requires travel like mine, but we all need a base of operations for whatever the Lord has for us. What will the physical location of your work by city, state, and nation be? If you'll be traveling to accomplish your goals, make a list of the general and/or specific places. This can be huge help for those whom the Lord is preparing to be of assistance to you. If someone has a purpose in England as you do, the Lord can use your purpose as a confirmation for that individual. That person may join with you for a time, or maybe permanently.

After you've fleshed out these six roots on your Destiny Overview, you must again ask yourself these questions:

+ Is this really what I believe the Lord has planned for me?

+ Am I passionate about this?

+ Can I give my life to this?

If you can't answer yes to these questions, then you need to go back to the Lord and ask Him to show you what the problem is. If changes are to be made, make them. And know this, even if your major and minor goals change as you go, your purpose will remain the same.

> "Your purpose is not what you aim for; it's your very reason for being. It creates your destiny."
> —*Bill Greenman*

FINAL THOUGHTS

When we ended our circus in 1989, it was with the understanding that I was to pursue the prophetic ministry full-time until further notice. Did my purpose change? No. Only my plans of how to walk it out. My goals were adjusted. My location was changed. My sphere of influence was very different. But I never received a word from the Lord that my *purpose* had changed. Knowing this is very freeing in the midst of radical changes.

This is the dichotomy of creating a Destiny Overview. We must prepare as if it will never change, yet always be ready to change at any moment—thus the word *overview*. But that's not a cause for confusion. God's not interested in keeping us on edge, making us wonder if we'll get to finish one thing before He changes His mind. If and when He redirects our path, He will make sure that our purpose will not change and that we will continue to fulfill the destiny He's set before us. He'll usually let us know in advance if He plans to make a change, giving us plenty of time to adjust. After all, He loves us.

> *For I am confident of this very thing, that He who began a good work in you will perfect it until the day of Christ Jesus.*
>
> (Philippians 1:6)

As you write out the foundational roots of your Destiny Overview, you'll be penning your future to a great extent. Take all the time necessary to formulate those roots. They'll be invaluable in creating a clear and concise plan for living out your purpose. In writing out your root system, you are creating goals. The clearer your goals, the easier it will be for you and those running with you to stay focused and on track to successful accomplishment.

In the next chapter, we'll discuss what goals are and how you can release their power for both your benefit and the benefit of others you'll encounter along your journey of fulfilling your purpose. We'll also discuss how to avoid the traps that goals can present.

10

GOD GOALS

*"I press on toward the goal for the prize of the upward call of
God in Christ Jesus."*
—Philippians 3:14

I've listened to dozens upon dozens of teachings on success, planning, motivation, and time management, and have read scores of books, including biographies of many great men and women. The one factor that's constant above all else is that of creating the invaluable skill of goal-setting. Goals from God will always be a part of our personal purpose, so why not get good at it?

Each successful person I've studied, interviewed, read about, listened to, or sought counsel with agrees that *goal-setting is not an option*; it is mandatory for high achievement. Fortunately, it's a skill that anyone can develop through diligent practice. Don't wait to begin creating goals; just get started, and the skill will come. As your proficiency increases, you'll spend less time setting goals and they'll be more measurable. So with this in mind, let's begin a short course in goal-setting.

"You only get the goals you set!"
—*Bill Greenman*

To set a goal, you have to know what you want. If you never decide what you want, then you won't have much more than what others give you—and that may not make you very happy. It certainly won't fulfill you. Goals are the stuff of life. They are our destiny, our future. Our individual purpose, destiny, and achievements are all subject to the goals we create in fulfilling them. That truth should be enough to make us all rabid goal-setters.

> "To get what you want, you must know what you want
> and passionately want what you want!"
> —*Anonymous*

When Jesus said, *"All things are possible to him who believes"* (Mark 9:23), He stated the two facts that make mankind different from any other being in creation.

Fact #1: You have the ability to believe in something before it happens.

Fact #2: You can accomplish whatever you believe will happen.

That is the "stuff" of goals! Goals spark us with hope. They kindle the flames of belief. They're not merely stepping-stones to something great; they are the very heart and soul of great things. Most of the time, the journey along the "goals path" is more important than the destination.

Earlier in this book, we mentioned that an individual without a personal purpose is doomed to perish, because he is unguided and unrestrained, without a cause higher than his own existence. What is a purpose? A vision? A revelation? Are they not goals? It's the destination of our purpose that captivates us and draws us through our lives with hope, curiosity, and excitement, and it's the goals within the vision that make up the days, weeks, years, and decades of life. You can't go on in this book, or with any power in your life for that matter, without a healthy love for goal-setting and goal-achieving. So, from this point on, I will assume that you have such a love and are eager to tap into the power inherent in goals.

The primary item needed for setting goals is a clearly defined *desire*. Ask yourself again what exactly you want. If you can't answer this question, then you can't set your goals. We have already discovered the groundwork of desire: It's your God-ordained purpose in this life. Once you know it, your goal-setting can begin. At the same time, don't be afraid to have desires from your own heart that are not directly part of your purpose. I firmly believe that if you're seeking the will of God with all your heart, you will not have, or at least give in to, desires that are out of line with the will of God for you.

ROADBLOCKS

Over the past several decades of setting and achieving goals, I've found that there are some common roadblocks that keep people from fulfilling their goals. I believe that if you have a proper understanding of these roadblocks, you'll have greater confidence to begin or complete the goals you need to fulfill your destiny. The following list has served me well over the years, and I've found similar lists among the volumes of books and courses I've studied. As you read through these roadblocks, I hope you are inspired by new possibilities in achieving your goals.

ROADBLOCK #1: FEAR OF FAILURE

Failing to complete a goal can be devastating and discouraging, but I believe that not attempting to set goals is far more dangerous. So if you know what causes the fear of failure to achieve goals, you can easily see them and avoid them. Hopefully this list of the top causes of fear of failure will help you avoid it.

Many people never set goals out of fear. First, they're afraid they'll never reach them! The fear of not accomplishing something you really desire is what the writer of Proverbs meant when he stated, *"Hope deferred makes the heart sick"* (Proverbs 13:12). Fear saps us of strength and crushes our joy. We've all experienced such setbacks, and the thought that we might have another one because of dreamy goal-setting can be unpleasant to say the least. But it's precisely when such thoughts pop up that we must take them *"captive to the obedience of Christ"* (2 Corinthians 10:5) and say, "I will do this thing! I will not be stopped! I will succeed!"

The second fear of failure is being afraid that we *will* reach our goals. I believe that this second fear is the more insidious of the first. Fear of success is actually *fear of change.* But change is what being a Christian is all about. It's about becoming a new creature, a new person in Christ who is constantly maturing in the ways of God's kingdom.

What we're really saying when we give in to these fears is that we're afraid God won't take care of us through the process of accomplishing these goals. When we can't trust God to change us, we usually have an unstable relationship with Him. But we *are* to become something we never were before, and that will require a lot of change! When we make Jesus Christ our Savior and Lord, we will experience change in our speech, our attitudes, our temperament, our thoughts, our friends, and many other things. Believe it or not, very little of this happens without our setting goals to make those changes.

Don't let Satan steal your dream at the goal level. Remember how much God loves you. Just as new parents are ready to catch their baby as he learns to take his first step, God's arms are outstretched to catch you should you fall. God's love compels Him to watch over you. He's more than able to take care of you.

ROADBLOCK #2: IRRESPONSIBILITY

Suffice it to say, you are ultimately responsible for setting your own goals and seeing them through. Finger-pointing is for the immature. Achieving your goals is up to you. God will help you all along the way, and if you need, help ask for it. Read books, take courses, do what it takes. You can.

ROADBLOCK #3: LACK OF KNOWLEDGE

Knowing the how-tos of something is vital. The Bible clearly states that God's *"people are destroyed for lack of knowledge"* (Hosea 4:6). If you don't know how to set and perform goals, you'll never do so, and therefore will achieve much less than what you'd achieve if you had the knowledge. How many discoveries have been postponed or perhaps lost completely because someone lacked the knowledge of how to set goals? Don't let a lack of knowledge in setting and accomplishing goals steal from you. Learn it. Get it in you! Be tenacious about gathering knowledge.

ROADBLOCK #4: NOT BELIEVING IN YOURSELF

This is a paralyzing state of mind. The moment we believe we can't, we won't! Whether our lack of confidence is based on fact or fiction, the results will be the same: nothing! We must believe the Scriptures, which say, *"I can do all things through* [Christ] *who strengthens me"* (Philippians 4:13) and, *"All things are possible"* (Matthew 19:26), because we believe in Jesus!

This failure has snared me the most. I wasn't a self-confident child, youth, or young man. Fortunately, my insecurity forced me to confront it. I realized that no one could help me until I did something about it. I didn't want to be a statistic in some magazine article on social dysfunction. Before I gave my life completely to Christ, I had to push myself past my insecurity. It wasn't easy doing this by myself, and I don't recommend it!

I pulled myself out from under the cloud of self-doubt through high-school sports and surfing. I learned to surf growing up in south Florida. Surfing was the best, because there was no competition. Progress was easy to see, and compliments were many from my surfing buddies. Scholastic sports were a different story, as I mentioned in chapter 4, "What's My Mix?" I had no apparent athletic gifts! However, attempting those sports did bring some recognition, even though it was mostly sympathy. But anything was better than nothing, and it was enough to boost my confidence to get me into college, where I excelled in martial arts and then the circus. Believe it or not, those two endeavors eventually led me into public ministry.

I read an article years ago that summarized my feelings on this subject of insecurity. Its conclusion was that if you're afraid to do something, just do it scared! I loved that! Just go and do whatever it is you want to do in spite of the fear. It was so freeing to me. So, when I read in a newspaper in April 1973 that male students were needed in Florida State University's Flying High Circus, my first thought was that I'd be embarrassed if I had trouble learning things like trapeze or juggling. But my second thought was, *Go give it a try anyway!* This actually set the course of my life for the next seventeen years. So don't be paralyzed by your personal lack of confidence; just do whatever it is you want to do scared! You won't regret it, even if you can't do as much as you had wanted.

ROADBLOCK #5: IMMEASURABLE GOALS

If you can't measure your progress, you'll never know close you are to finishing a goal. An athlete's practice sessions allow him to measure his progress, seeing how much closer he is to his best time, longest jump, farthest throw, and so forth. And wouldn't it be foolish to run a business without some sort of record-keeping to see if you're gaining or losing money, clients, and assets? You simply have to set goals to track your progress toward achievement. Knowing that you are making progress will fuel confidence and vision for more achievement.

There are two types of goals—measurable and immeasurable. Measurable goals are those you can actually see taking place, such as building bigger muscles, earning more money, or getting a new job. You can touch, taste, see, hear, or smell a measurable goal. Immeasurable goals are things like becoming stronger in your Christian faith or increasing in your ability to make decisions. You can't feel these types of goals being accomplished, even though they are just as real as the ones you can see and touch.

The goal of building a circus to preach the gospel of Jesus Christ was a measurable goal. The goal to gain control of my anger was an immeasurable goal. Regardless of the type, both measurable and immeasurable goals can still be tracked by setting smaller, minor goals along the way to achieving them.

TASKS

Each goal you have must be broken down into small, measurable, bitesized goals, also called tasks, for easier accomplishment. This will allow you to both project years into the future (your destiny) yet begin working on them today. You must decide on a main goal and then begin to plan for it by finding the first, and then the next and the next. I've set major goals and their many tasks in both business and ministry, sometimes decades before I started to see any progress, but I have seen many come to pass almost overnight. And though I often have no idea when some tasks that are out of my control will be done, I do know I'll be prepared when their time comes. That's a real confidence builder!

THE MOTIVATORS

Now that we've seen some of the hinderances to setting and accomplishing our goals, let's look at what really makes them fly into reality. These are what I call "The Motivators"—the engines of our goal and destiny achievement. They keep us moving forward when others fall away.

MOTIVATION

Motivation's a strange concept. It's amazing what can motivate people. Some are motivated by money, others by things, others by love or hate. Some people are motivated by sheer will, while others are motivated by fear. But there's only one motivating factor that can stand the test and trials of life. It isn't directed by our long-term needs, wants, or fears. It's the one factor that no one can stop and has sent men to conquer the unconquerable and win the unwinnable. The number one motivating power in life: *belief in something higher than oneself.*

A person empowered by belief—be it a quest, an assignment, a person, or a pipe dream—is unstoppable.

+ When Goliath taunted Israel, it was the belief of a teenage boy that killed him!

+ When racial segregation seemed unstoppable, Martin Luther King Jr.'s belief in equality led the African-American community to ignore the dangers and change the nation.

+ Belief pushed Christopher Columbus past the limits of the known world and brought him back to his land with the discovery of a new land on the maps for all to explore after him.

+ Belief led Nelson Mandela to endure decades of prison and anguish to see the end of apartheid in South Africa and change the hearts of people worldwide.

+ Belief led Thomas Edison to attempt over one thousand experiments before he illuminated the world with the incandescent lightbulb.

+ Belief motivated the greatest act of love ever displayed, when Christ Jesus gave up His life for the lives of all who went before Him and would come after Him.

There is no stronger motivator than belief.

"Motivation is a fire from within.
If someone else tries to light that fire under you,
chances are it will burn very briefly."
—*Stephen Covey*

Temporary thrills or perishable things rarely motivate some-one for a lifetime. Goals alone are poor motivators. *"The prize of the high calling of God in Christ Jesus"* (Philippians 3:14 KJV) is to be our motivation, no matter how He asks us to live it out. It's the only motivation that can keep us focused and fulfilled for a lifetime.

There's amazing power in believing. Scientific studies have shown that belief can actually change human biochemistry. Researchers have given volunteers strong depressant drugs but told them that they were powerful stimulants. Because these people believed the scientists, their bodies began to create the very drugs they thought they were receiving! What each person believed over-rode the fact that they had taken depressant drugs. This was not mind over matter but mind *manipulating* matter!

For as [a man] thinketh in his heart, so is he.

(Proverbs 23:7 KJV)

THE SOURCE OF OUR MOTIVATION

"The stronger the 'why,' the easier the 'how.'"
—*Anonymous*

The whys of your life must be bigger than you. They have to be more valuable than you. They have to be more worthy than you. As

I noted at the beginning of this book, they must glorify God and help people. If this is the case, the "how" will be easier to endure.

You're motivated more by what you believe than by any other aspect of your being. A man filled with the desire to serve God is aware that the source of his belief is, at the same time, the object of his quest: namely, the will of God for him personally. Know what you believe. Guard your heart and mind from beliefs that are not firmly grounded in the will and the Word of God. It's there that your belief is coupled with the supernatural power of our Lord Jesus.

BENEFITS

Many times, the completion of a goal is all the reward you need. But God understands what motivates people and He isn't against rewarding achievers. David was motivated by anger that Goliath defied the armies of Israel, the nation who had a covenant with God, but also by the bounty of the rewards. In fact, it was so interesting to him that he asked about it more than once before he went into battle.

Everything we accomplish has benefits or rewards beyond the actual achievement itself. These benefits spread out as you achieve more and more, creating a sort of ripple effect. Drop a pebble into a pond and before long the ripples will touch every drop of the water's surface and every inch of the shoreline. So it is with reaching the goals in our life areas. There's little you will achieve in one area of life that doesn't affect the other areas, bringing more glory to God and helping more people, while changing you for the better. That's the economy of God. When He ordains our purpose, He makes sure that as many people as possible get blessed through us!

To this end, I've placed three columns pertaining to the rewards and benefits on the "Destiny Goals" worksheet in the *Purpose Master Planner.* This worksheet allows you to keep not only your goals but also their benefits before you for added motivation.

Be sure that your benefits list is not filled in solely with what rewards *you*. God and people should be the priorities of our lives. Although God is definitely interested in our pleasure, He also wants us to share the wealth with our fellow man. Benefits need not be merely temporal, either. Our goals should point to a purpose and destiny that extend beyond the limits of our personal life.

We should look for the benefits we generate to reach at least two generations beyond our own. Proverbs exhorts us to leave an inheritance for our children and our children's children (see Proverbs 13:22), but I personally have no intention of stopping there. My purpose dictates the production of materials that will be timeless in nature and just as relevant in two hundred years as they are the day I publish them. Look past your own time and see history holding a long-term place for your accomplishments.

> "Goals give you the specific direction to take to make
> your dreams come true."
> —*Bob Conklin*

GOAL YOUR LIFE

YOUR LIFE AREAS

These life areas are the same ones you used as categories when you made your dream list in chapter 5. Now you must commit to setting definite goals in these areas if you wish to see your dreams and desires fulfilled. Over the years, I've found that few people think about these areas as actual segments of their lives that *require* goals and plans. Consequently, they suffer in the areas they don't create goals. Don't fall short of the benefits that your goals will produce.

THE HALF-DOZEN RULE

I've mentioned this before, but it bears repeating here. Although you can have many goals under each life area, it's better to keep the number small for easier control and accomplishment. This is consistent with what I call the "half-dozen rule," which states that everything you want to learn or master can be achieved through about a half-dozen goals. These are the basics, the fundamentals—just like the master principles.

Master these disciplines before you set specific goals in a life area. For example, if your goal is to be a worship leader, then you first master a lifestyle of worship. If your goal is to own assets of one million dollars, then you must master the basics of budgeting, saving, and investing. If your goal is to be an Olympic champion, then you must master the basics of good nutrition, exercise, and rest. Your success depends on your diligence with the half-dozen basics.

Here's a list of some basics for each life area. But by doing these, you'll find yourself discovering others.

1. *Spirit* – Be involved in Bible study; prayer; worship; fellowship; giving; witnessing.

2. *Intellect* – Practice decisiveness; thinking on purpose; taking your thoughts captive to the obedience of Christ (see 2 Corinthians 10:5); and meditating on the Word of God (see Psalm 1; Joshua 1:8).

3. *Personality* - Be passionate; humble; full of integrity; kind; serving; confident; vulnerable; and have a positive attitude.

4. *Physical* – Practice good nutrition; exercise; rest/sleep; hygiene; and stress reduction.

5. *People* – Live intentionally with family members; friends; coworkers; neighbors; community; and other believers.

6. *Money* – Create a budget; tithe; be generous; save; insurance; investments.

Just pick one item in one heading at a time, then set your goals and go after them. If you *diligently* perform these simple tasks, your life will dramatically change for the better and you'll be well on your way to attaining any goals you set!

"Inch by inch, anything's a cinch!"
—*Robert Schuller*

CONGRUENT GOALS

Every goal of each life area should form a complementary chain with those in other areas. Simply check your personal goals and see if they all point in the same direction—your destiny's direction. If you find that any of them don't, take them before the Lord and discuss them. You can't afford to be sidetracked or misguided by incongruent goals.

This doesn't mean that you can't have goals that are *not* directly in line with your purpose. For instance, I have goals that entail some rather adventurous endeavors, like whitewater rafting and surfing. They also happen to be a lot of fun, and God loves it when I have fun. If you've ever seen the movie *Chariots of Fire*, you might remember Eric Lidell's famous line: "When I run, I feel [God's] pleasure." That's how I feel when I do those types of things.

"Winners make goals; losers make excuses."
—*Anonymous*

ALWAYS FOLLOW THROUGH

Finish what you start. We've talked a lot about goals and the things we need to know to make them happen. Coming up with goals is great, but doing them is the pathway to success. That takes determination. You have to be committed to the follow-through, from start to finish. Lip service means nothing; action is everything. Decide you won't quit no matter what gets in your way. And if you hit some roadblocks, be patient. Figure out the detour or wait till the path clears. And remember that God is with you on the goal journey. You are never alone!

FINAL THOUGHTS

I don't want you to be overwhelmed by the prospect of having to know or do everything I've shared in this chapter. But do consider the fact that you won't fulfill your purpose or live the destiny you were meant to live without a clear commitment to formulating and carrying out the goals necessary to get you there. Life doesn't just happen; you won't just happen to achieve the accomplishments ordained for you by the Lord.

You must take the bull of your future by the horns, look it squarely in the eyes, and tell it where you want to go and how you expect to get there. If you can hold on to that picture, that commitment, then you will go farther than you ever dreamed possible! You'll accomplish more than the majority of your peers. You'll be in demand by those wanting to do the same. Next, we'll cover the how-tos of turning your goals into productive plans.

11

WHAT ABOUT PLANNING?

"I will study, I will prepare, and my time will come."
—Abraham Lincoln

If there's one place people fall down in the pursuit of their purpose, it's in the area of planning. Planning sounds mundane, tedious, and just plain boring. But if you can grasp the big picture of what planning can do for every area of your life—how it can motivate, stimulate, and inspire your daily endeavors—you'll change your mind about the negatives and embrace the positives of this vital master principle.

THE POWER OF PLANNING

In 1953, the entire graduating class of Yale University was interviewed. The results of that interview revealed that only 3 percent of the graduates of this Ivy League institution had any plans written down for accomplishing their life goals. That shocked me when I read it—this is Yale we're talking about! Two decades later, the interviewer searched for and found the interviewed graduates strewn across the world in various occupations. He asked them the same questions, and his findings this time were even more surprising than those in the first interview!

A full twenty years after having written down their goals and how they would accomplish them, the same 3 percent were light-years ahead of the pack—just as they had been in 1953. By comparison, the other 97 percent were greatly lacking. The 3 percent were now worth more financially than the entire 97 percent combined! They had more self-esteem and felt more fulfilled than their counterparts (what a surprise!). They had chosen to plan what they desired and then went to work on doing those plans.

My question to you is, Which group do *you* want to be in?

MY OWN PILGRIMAGE

As a six-year-old child, I began to set goals for my own life (sort of). The first was when I was in kindergarten and had been appointed Master of Ceremonies for the class Christmas pageant. My job consisted of leading a very short parade of classmates around the small stage and then bowing before the enthralled audience of assembled parents and siblings. As I bowed that night in December 1959, something wonderful happened. As a thunderous round of applause resounded in the room, in my little kindergarten heart I knew that this was what I wanted to do with my life—make people smile and clap when I did something on a stage!

From that moment on, I began to pursue what has become my life's work: performing for others. Of course, it's taken many different paths, but the gist of my work has always been to make people smile. Through the years, this desire manifested itself on grade-school stages and high-school athletic fields, at Boy Scout events, and at surfing spots up and down the East Coast of the U.S. (and even Hawaii). I've performed in literally hundreds of circus performances under canvas tents and steel-beamed arenas,

sung in church services and plays, and even been a master illusion-
ist at one of the largest theme parks in America. I'm still living that
dream every time I teach a seminar or minister on this finding
your purpose and other life-changing subjects around the world.

> "Even the best team, without a plan, can't score."
> —*Coach John Wooden*

JESUS' EXAMPLE

I've been asked if I thought Jesus and the disciples had some
grandiose planning system as they wandered about the country-
side preaching the good news. I believe that they absolutely planned
ahead. Jesus was responsible for a home in Capernaum; traveled
with twelve men He had to train and feed; covered a lot of terrain in
three years of ministry excursions; kept His treasurer busy by giving
to the poor and paying for His expenses; fed five thousand and later
four thousand people in two different settings with very specific and
orderly instructions; and held to a prayer time every morning before
the sun rose. You don't accomplish those kinds of would-be scheduling nightmares without some very good plans in place!

Okay, but did He have anything written down? Absolutely—
before time and till the end of time! His entire life was planned
by the Father to culminate on the cross and in His resurrection.
Also, the names of all who have made and will make Jesus Christ
the Lord of their lives are already written in the Lamb's Book of
Life. Nothing was or is a surprise. Everything has happened and
is happening according to prophesy hundreds of years before. *That*
is first-rate planning!

If you really mean business with your purpose, you'll have to put
on your planner's hat and rise to the next level of goal-setting. No goal,

dream, or desire will be fulfilled in any expedient, lasting way without a proactive, productive plan to make it so. You have to believe that.

> *The plans of the diligent lead surely to advantage, but every-one who is hasty comes surely to poverty.*   (Proverbs 21:5)

What do I mean by "proactive"? Being proactive means that you are on the aggressive side of planning. You do not wait for someone to come along with a plan for you. You take the offensive. Proactive means that your are up before the sun and have the day planned before it dawns! It means that your future is no surprise, because you already have the events on paper. It means that you are ready and waiting instead of surprised and wailing.

As one person man said, "Fail to plan and you plan to fail." Planning begins when our own minds and imaginations come into contact with the divine thoughts of God. It is there in the union of spirit and mind that God can paint the picture of His will upon the canvas of our hearts. It's a supernatural exchange but often does not feel supernatural. In fact, we're all so used to such imagining that we can easily miss much Holy-Spirit-inspired information if we aren't listening. (This is where knowing the language of the Holy Spirit really comes into play!) Now I want to share with you a dynamic technique for tapping into the thoughts of God.

PRIME THE PUMP

> *A plan in the heart of a man is like deep water, but a man of understanding draws it out.*   (Proverbs 20:5)

> *Watch over your heart with all diligence, for from it flow the springs of life.*   (Proverbs 4:23)

If your plans are in your heart and your heart is like deep water, just how are you to pull them out? After asking that question while praying one day, I recalled a memory of when I was a young boy at our house on Song Lake in upstate New York. I had been with some other children in the backyard on a hot summer day, and we had been trying feverishly to make an old, red hand-crank water pump give up its water—to no avail. Each of us had tried with all our might, but all we'd gotten for our efforts was a raspy squeak from the rusted crank handle.

Then my father had appeared and performed what seemed like magic to us. He'd had a large glass jar filled with water and had emptied its contents into the old red pump. While he poured, he'd firmly and rhythmically worked the handle up and down. Suddenly, to our wide-eyed amazement, cool water began to pour out of the old pump in a steady flow from its underground source somewhere deep below our feet. We'd cupped our hands and drank and splashed one another other for a few minutes as my father smiled and pumped away. Then, as we were settling down again and were about to ask him how he'd gotten the water to come out, he'd answered our question. "Son, if you want water from the well, you've gotta prime the pump first."

As the memory faded, I understood what the Lord was trying to tell me! It was the seed/harvest principle again. If I wanted to draw the plans from within my heart for the goals I was setting, I first had to *prime the pump*! The law of seed and harvest states that, to get oranges, you must plant orange seeds. To get apples, you must plant apple seeds. So, to get plans, which are nothing more than ideas and thoughts, I had to plant thoughts and ideas! How simple! All I had to do to get the plans for anything I needed was to take the time to meditate, daydream, and think about the very goals I needed plans for, and then the plans would come up from the depth of my heart. And you know what? It worked!

All you need to do is give yourself some quiet time, space, and relaxation. Let your mind and body relax and ask the Holy Spirit to help you concentrate on the goal you wish to plan. Begin to picture the goal from the beginning to the end and all the points in between. But begin with a question.

START WITH A QUESTION

Why start with a question? Questions are the cleanest water with which to prime the pump of your being. They spark the ultimate thoughts of ignition. When you ask yourself a question, your mind instantly goes to work to answer it. That makes your subconscious mind go to work, too. Your subconscious will automatically begin to file through every memory and every bit of information in your brain to answer the question put before it. At the same time, you'll open your spirit to receive input from the Lord.

Remember, "*The spirit of man is the lamp of the* Lord, *searching all the innermost parts of his being*" (Proverbs 20:27). God will touch your spirit with illuminating ideas and plans. It may astound you how many answers bubble up when you do this. But be sure to let your mind first receive those answers without judging. Attempting to qualify each thought, picture, or idea will stifle the flow. Just let the ideas and thoughts flow and write them down.

A final thought on priming the pump. The more often a pump is used, the less water is needed to prime it. Therefore, once you get into the habit of priming the pump of your imagination with thoughts and questions, your needed information will flow out with less effort. Get into the habit of priming your mental and spiritual pump on a daily basis—on purpose. Take time each day, or several times a day, to daydream and get the flow started. Then you'll discover that the flow of ideas and information you need will pop up even when you're not trying to acquire any! And be sure to write down what you receive!

However, you can't just cover a piece of paper with ideas on how you'd *like* something to be done. Once the ideas begin to flow, you must be sure they'll produce what you want. That requires a proven, workable planning system, one that works every time for everything and for everybody. Studying planning over the past four decades, I eventually came up with a system that works for me. It's simple yet covers all the bases.

THE SIX UNIVERSAL RESOURCES

Every goal you ever attempt to achieve will require the help of one or more of the "six universal resources." (Remember the half-dozen rule.) There is nothing mystical about these resources. They are basic, practical, and easily understood by anyone.

Before I explain them, let me state that they're very broad. By that I mean that there may be literally hundreds of items under any one of these headings that go into meeting a single goal. For instance, when I had to plan large conventions and concerts, I'd have a wide variety of equipment to rent and scores of people to place, but needed very few soft supplies. In other words, don't be misled by the small number of headings and think for a moment that you should have the same number of items for each goal. This list is a a general outline for you to fill in for every step in your plan. By using this list, you can assure yourself that you will run into very few surprises along the way, because you know exactly what to expect and when to expect it.

Also, in your *Purpose Master Planner*, you'll find a "Master Resources" worksheet. Make copies of this chart and use it for anything you ever plan. This indespensible review form lists all six resources and is easy to use. I've used it for over three decades with great success, and there are literally thousands of people around the globe using it and experiencing similar results.

RESOURCE #1: PEOPLE

There's no doubt that your most valuable resource is the people you'll need for the fulfillment of each and every goal. Forget the idea that you are a Lone Ranger, an island unto yourself. You need people to help you do whatever your purpose is, and every step along the path of your destiny will require interaction with others in some manner. This is not a maybe; it's a guarantee! And be sure to see others as equal in value. Never use people just to accomplish something. Relationships are at the heart of God. He created us to have a family, and He commands us to love one another as He loves us. That includes everyone you'll work with as you live out your plans, goals, and fulfill your destiny.

RESOURCE #2: FACILITY

When talking of facilities, you have to consider every possible building or the piece of land you may need to accomplish your goal. Ask the question, "What will I need to do in this area?" In a facility, you might need restrooms, offices, board rooms, food areas, and more. For our circus, we used a wide variety of facilities, which depended on the town, the sponsor, and the event of which we were a part. We couldn't afford to arrive at the show site unaware of the facility, because we had to plan the proper rigging to put on our show. Each venue afforded its own problems and challenges, but we knew these details in advance because we had to complete the planning chart in advance.

RESOURCE #3: EQUIPMENT

This is the precise hardware you will need to accomplish your goals. Ask the question, "What equipment do I need to achieve this particular goal?" Then simply let your mind go to work. Computers, copiers, backhoes, trucks, sound systems, volley-balls—whatever fits the goal.

RESOURCE #4: SUPPLIES

Supplies refer to anything consumable, things that you will use up and/or eventually discard. Simply think of all the items that will need to be replaced after you are done reaching your goal, and write them in the "Supplies" column. For the circus, we had a fairly constant flow of supplies. Items such as adhesive tape for wrapping wrists and ankles; pine rosin for keeping our hands dry while catching people in midair; paper for copies and letters; envelopes; stamps; food and drink for the troupe; gas for the trucks; light bulbs; and so forth—and all such were consumable supplies.

RESOURCE #5: COST

Nothing is free…well, usually. This being true, why are most people so reluctant to preplan their spending? Why do so many new businesses in America fail? Why are so many people hopelessly in debt with credit cards and bank loans? I'm not sure I know all the answers, but the main reasons are usually due to either ignorance or laziness. You have to count the cost of all things pertaining to whatever you are planning—whatever is under all the other resources.

RESOURCE #6: TIME

Projecting deadlines, the completion dates, requires accurate knowledge of what is needed to achieve each specific item. You will need calendars, and be sure to use them! Make a full timeline for the overall project and include each task for each goal. In this area of timing is where most mistakes are made, as we saw in chapter 8, "Know That You Know."

If you don't control how you spend your time, someone or something else will fill that void for you—and not necessarily in a positive way. The truth is, if you know what your goals are and you have figured out your resources, their costs, and who you need to help you, you are light-years ahead of the pack and ready for time management. The point is to simply set realistic time frames for each aspect of each goal—be it the acquisition of a piece of equipment or the networking of a new person to help you.

"Your will to prepare must exceed your will to win."
—*Bill Greenman*

THE FINAL STEP IN PLANNING YOUR DESTINY

Commit your works to the LORD and your plans will be estab-lished....The mind of man plans his way, but the LORD directs his steps. (Proverbs 16:3, 9)

All the planning in the world is futile if it's not submitted to the lordship of Christ. Yes, we must plan. Yes, we must set and work toward our goals. Yes, we must unflinchingly commit our-selves to the task. But that commitment, that work, must never block out the One for whom is meant all the glory of our achieve-ments. Plans are written by us, but their establishment is *His* responsibility. Actually, this releases us from the fear of relying on our own finite understanding to make our destiny plans take place. You must be willing to let God's timing for the sequence of events take precedence over your own.

FINAL THOUGHTS

If I was going to build a house, I'd want the most detailed plans I could get my hands on. The last thing I'd want would be a wall through the kitchen sink drain or my chimney on one side of the house and the fireplace on another! We'd call that "big league" ignorance! But how many of us have been guilty of doing just that with our destiny? We fail to plan, and then we just plain fail! Or we plan without the proper tools, and we end up taking years longer to accomplish our goals than we should have, if we accom-plish them at all.

No carpenter worth his hire would even think about going to his job without everything he needed to do the job right—plans, tools, helpers, and supplies. Shouldn't we be just as professional with our lives for the Lord Jesus? Of course. So then, once we understand planning and commit all our plans to the Lord, then we must get to work in some very specific ways.

MASTER PRINCIPLE #3

LIVE YOUR DESTINY

"Prepare your minds for action."
—1 Peter 1:13

"Prove yourselves doers of the word."
—James 1:22

Once you have the plans and you understand what your purpose is and how to accomplish it, then you have to go do it. But there are specific ways that are much more profound than just "doing" things. In the following chapters, I'll give you some tools that will help you get started. Achievement—consistant achievement—is certainly an acquired skill. It's a master principle. When you know the techniques of achievement, you can apply them to anything, and applying them to your purpose is a must.

12

THAT'S IN MY HEAD?

"Thinking is the catalyst of the creative process."
—*Bill Greenman*

Therefore I urge you, brethren, by the mercies of God, to present your bodies a living and holy sacrifice, acceptable to God, which is your spiritual service of worship. And do not be conformed to this world, but **be transformed** *by the renewing of your mind, so that you may prove what the will of God is, that which is good and acceptable and perfect. For through the grace given to me I say to everyone among you not to think more highly of himself than he ought to think; but to think so as to have sound judgment, as God has allotted to each a measure of faith.* (Romans 12:1–3)

Do not eat the bread of a selfish man, or desire his delicacies; for as he **thinks** *within himself, so he is ["as he thinketh in his heart, so is he" (*KJV*)].* (Proverbs 23:6–7)

AS A MAN THINKS

You are today what you thought yesterday, and tomorrow you'll become what you think today. If you're not satisfied with who you are and what you want, then you'll have to change your thinking. Transformation is forever linked with changed thinking. It's a law that always works, so why not put it to work for you? I have no doubt that if you've read the previous chapters, you have already begun to rethink your thinking.

Be careful what you think about. Be sure that you are always filling your thought-life with worthy topics—subjects you wish to take part in and to become a part of you. Be careful whom you associate with, for their thinking may not be what you desire. You must constantly ask yourself whether the people you are associating with are thinking in line with your purpose and destiny, and whether the thoughts you entertain in their presence are in line, as well.

Our thinking very powerfully affects our purpose and destiny, and it will drive our achievement. We must set a much higher standard than what is set by most of those around us. We must think in the realm of infinite possibilities. This is no small task, and I guarantee that you'll undergo vast positive, creative change when you enlist it. Embrace change! Seek it! Love it! It will always serve you for the better.

"For My thoughts are not your thoughts, nor are your ways My ways," declares the LORD. "For as the heavens are higher than the earth, so are My ways higher than your ways and My thoughts than your thoughts. For as the rain and the snow come down from heaven, and do not return there without watering the earth and making it bear and sprout, and furnishing seed to the sower and bread to the eater; so will My word be which goes forth from My mouth; it will not return to Me empty, without accomplishing what I desire, and

without succeeding in the matter for which I sent it."
(Isaiah 55:8–11)

A man's ways are dictated by how he thinks. Henry Ford's immortal words ring true for every man: "The man who thinks he can and the man who thinks he can't are both right." This is a paraphrase of King Solomon's declaration that as a man thinks, so is he. There is no denying it! There is, however, a way to enjoy it. Allow yourself to go beyond the limits of your past and the limits others place on you. Step into the realm of infinite possibilities.

"Focus your thinking and learning on whatever your personal purpose demands that you know, and you will be transformed into another and more valuable person."
—*Bill Greenman*

FOCUS IS JOB NUMBER ONE

You must focus your thoughts on your purpose. Don't be a flood lamp in this respect; be a laser beam! Concentrate your thoughts along the single line of your destiny until they burn right through to its achievement! Take every thought captive to the obedience of Christ's purpose. (See 2 Corinthians 10:5.) Don't let your unrestrained thoughts distract you as you pursue your life's mission. This is the secret of the most sucessful people in every field I've ever researched. No matter the occupation or calling, every great leader and highly productive person has been totally focused on his or her end result. I have also found it to be true in everything to which I've applied it.

+ Jesus kept *"the joy set before Him* [and] *endured the cross"* (Hebrews 12:2).

+ The apostle Paul was continually "[pressing] *on toward the goal for the prize of the upward call of God in Christ Jesus*" (Philippians 3:14).

To truly excel in your purpose, to truly achieve the maximum, you must be focused on your destination. By keeping your mind locked onto your destiny, you'll be virtually unstoppable!

IMPROVE YOUR SKILLS

Do you see a man skilled in his work? He will stand before kings; he will not stand before obscure men.

(Proverbs 22:29)

You can't afford to be fragmented in your direction. You must develop skills primarily in the area of your purpose. It is the skilled person, the masterful individual, who dominates an industry and/or accomplishes the impossible.

When God planned the building of the tabernacle in the wilderness after freeing Israel from slavery, He called for the skilled craftsmen to do the work, not just anyone who wanted to volunteer. Then, after the workers came forward for the task, He *blessed* their skills even more by His Holy Spirit. (See Exodus 31:1–6.) A Christian who is constantly improving his or her skills will enjoy the presence of the Lord more. It's part of our stewardship to continually develop our gifts and skills in the areas God calls us to.

It's the skilled person who will stand before the kings of this world. It goes without saying that no king would summon a common, unlearned man into his chambers for counsel or service. So why be common when you can excel before kings! I plan to be one who fulfills that challenge, by developing skills that are both appreciated and needed by leaders. Not in a prideful way, or for my exaltation, but in a way that will help the people they lead, whom God wants to reach with His love and the gospel of Christ.

For me, this means continued research in the areas affecting my purpose, destiny, and achievement. It means improving my speaking and writing techniques. It means developing more skill in consulting and management to help people and businesses develop their visions. It requires me to be trained in finances and health, so that I can continue to travel and produce more educational materials. I want my skills to still be growing in these areas when I reach my nineties!

> "More knowledge is little help to him who has yet to act
> on what he already knows."
> —*Bill Greenman*

The prudent are crowned with knowledge.
                                        (Proverbs 14:18 KJV)

The mind of the intelligent seeks knowledge. (Proverbs 15:14)

The mind of the prudent acquires knowledge, and the ear of the wise seeks knowledge.   (Proverbs 18:15)

There are over two hundred references to knowledge, understanding, and wisdom in the book of Proverbs. God obviously wants us to know their importance, but it must not stop there. Skill must come from that knowledge. Data is not the issue; knowing what to do with data is the issue.

TAPPING INTO THE WEALTH OF ROLE MODELS

#1: FIND MENTORS

When I want to learn something new or enhance a skill, I first seek out someone who already has such skills. I observe this person for a while, and learn all I can from a spectator's point of view. Then I go to that person, if possible, and ask him if he will allow me to directly learn from him. I'm up-front and honest about it. I offer to give back something in return, such as time, effort, or money. I can't remember anyone turning me down, and I've made sure not to turn down anyone who asks the same of me.

Next, I spend as much time with that person as I possibly can. I try to live in his hip pocket, so to speak. I continually ask questions. I take notes when necessary. I become a dutiful student by applying what he shares with me.

My strategy at this point is to estimate the time it will take me to learn the skills that my role model has spent years learning. I realize that I'll still need to put in the hours to achieve particular skills, but I know that I can also avoid many of the trials and errors my mentor endured by learning from his experiences. A mentor becomes a sort of educational "minesweeper" for me—removing the unseen and unknown time-consuming mistakes for me, so I can achieve the same skills in a shorter period of time.

I used this "role-modeling" technique to learn my slack wire act in the circus. I sought out the best wire walker at FSU, and he consented to help me learn his secrets and give me his valuable time in private sessions. I later did the same for those who came to me. When I stepped into the ministry, I applied the same technique with my pastor. I went everywhere with him, even in the middle of the night to pray for the sick on emergency calls. I did the same to get my black belts in the martial arts, and in becoming a skilled speaker and teacher.

The point is, whatever you want to do, go find a role model who's already an expert at it and copy that person as much as possible. Discover every one of his secrets and mistakes; then act accordingly with the information. Refuse to associate with anyone who does not think in terms of tremendous achievement. Surround yourself with the top achievers in each field.

"Do you want to achieve great things and fulfill your destiny? Then sow that kind of seed into your spirit, soul, and
body through associating with those who have cut the path!"
—*Bill Greenman*

#2: STUDY

When I wanted to write a book, I called writers. When I
wanted to sing, I spent time with singers. When I wanted to learn
to surf, I paddled out into the ocean and hung around with the
best! It was always worth my effort and time. But there were also
times when I couldn't find any mentors to spend time with. The
people I wanted to learn from were hundreds or thousands of
miles away, and I had no way to establish relationships. So I did
the next best thing—I studied their materials.

Find every book written by the mentor you want to learn from.
Allow experts you may never meet to teach you everything they know!
Do you have a computer with Web access or a library card? Did you
know that only about 3 percent of Americans have a library card?
(That's probably the same 3 percent found in the Yale class of 1953
who made plans for their goals!) The knowledge of the world is waiting for us on the Web and in the library, and oftentimes at no charge.

I've spent hours studying the works of those before me. Books
are literal storehouses of skill. Tap into the source of any skill you
need, and change your life. You'll feel smarter just surfing the Web
or walking around a library! Think of them as free universities
open 6/7 days a week just for you!

Become someone of consequence! Every great person I've
studied has proven the adage "Leaders are readers." Whatever
your purpose, your destiny should be filled with time in the books
on related topics. Create your own library and begin to stock it

with a legacy of insight and educational wonder that your inheritors will love you for.

Invest in your mind! Be sure that you don't spend more on movies and coffee than you do on books and training materials. Pass on going out for dinner, and purchase a book and stay home! Enroll for seminars in your area of purpose. Buy training courses that will enhance your skill. What you can't find in the library or online, buy in a bookstore. If you're frugal like me, you will find a half-price bookstore, which offers the best stuff at the best prices! I've found some gold mines of information for mere pennies in those stores. Just believe the fact that you are worth the investment. I don't believe there's a better dollar-for-dollar purchase than a book or an e-course.

Be a reader! Be a perpetual learner! Be a student for life and of life! See your purpose and destiny as an ongoing college or graduate level course, and never cease to seek more knowledge and wisdom for it. It's been said that if you want to be a local expert on something, read about one hundred books on the subject. If you want to be a national expert, read about seven hundred books on the subject. I average about two books (in parts), ten audios, and six or more Web site articles per week in the areas of my purpose. Why not go for it!

Here are two projects to help you tap into the wealth of role models on your way to achievement. You may need to visit a library to complete these tasks. If so, go do it and know that you are stepping into the 3 percent group of top achievers!

Project #1: **Make a list of the top ten people with skills pertaining to your purpose, whom you'd like to learn from (in person or otherwise).**

Project #2: **If applicable, make a list of the specific books or other learning materials produced by the people on your top-ten list that you'll need to get the necessary knowledge and skills to fulfill your purpose.**

Taking advantage of mentors and their teaching products are very helpful in ensuring success. But there will come a time when you must take the next step, which is to go beyond your mentors.

FINAL THOUGHTS: THE EXPANSION PROCESS

The expansion process is simply looking at all the knowledge and skills you have accumulated and then asking yourself what you can do to go beyond it all. I continually ask myself, "What more is there beyond the books, the teachings, and the skills I see in my mentors?" (I'm still working on this!) In marriage, I ask, "How can I be a more effective husband?" In parenting, I ask, "How can I be a better father?" (I'm really working on these!) When learning my wire act at FSU, I created new tricks, some never done before or since to my knowledge. And in ministry, I sought new ways to serve people and to teach what I had learned.

Furthermore, when I asked myself how I could go beyond my first book and teaching on purpose, destiny, and achievement, I developed a vision large enough to last my lifetime! The more I think this way and pursue those thoughts, the more I realize how small my thinking can be at time. The possibilities are almost limitless—especially when you remember that the Creator of the universe is there to help you!

> "Our personal purpose should be so large
> that we can't see an end to it."
> —*Bill Greenman*

And now that you understand how to keep your thoughts ever growing and expand your vision, you have to learn how to use the big three master principles, which will bring them into full manifestation.

13

MY BIG THREE
MASTER PRINCIPLES

"All things are possible to him who believes."
—Mark 9:23

"I can do all things through Him who strengthens me."
—Philippians 4:13

Within these two verses is the motto of my life. When I first read these verses in 1977, I realized that no matter what I wanted to do, I could do it; no matter where I wanted to go, I could go; and no matter whom I wanted to meet, learn from, or give to, I could do so! I instantly believed what I read in those Scriptures. And what I believe, I go after with everything I've got. It was the power locked within those truths that catapulted me into achieving my dreams of creating a professional and evangelistic circus; sustaining a happy, lasting marriage; raising God-loving children; writing my first book; having my own highly successful network marketing organizations; and all the other dreams that I have pursued.

IT'S NOT IMPOSSIBLE!

I want to take you from merely thinking about impossibilities to actually experiencing them. In this chapter, I'm going to lay out a master principle system for achieving virtually anything you wish. This system is comprised of three universal laws that have been proven around the world, in all cultures, for thousands of years—even though they are kingdom truths. That's the way of laws—they work for everyone. My focus here will be to reveal the power of these laws so that you use this system every day for your specific purpose.

> "Never make excuses; make a difference."
> —*Anonymous*

MY BIG THREE MASTER PRINCIPLES

There are three *main* master principles you must become skillful with. They have the power to open nearly every door to every area of your life. But, as with all principles, you must know how to use them…and then actually use them. I want you to begin to live with complete confidence, to open your heart to the unlimited possibilities of achievement, and to live your purpose to the fullest.

BIG MASTER PRINCIPLE #1: SEE IT

> "The world of tomorrow belongs to the person who has
> the vision for today."
> —*Robert Schuller*

And Jesus answered saying to them, "Have faith in God. Truly I say to you, whoever says to this mountain, 'Be taken up and

cast into the sea,' and does not doubt in his heart, but believes
that what he says is going to happen, it will be granted him.
Therefore I say to you, all things for which you pray and ask,
believe that you have received them, and they will be granted
you."   (Mark 11:22–24)

If you want to receive something from the Lord, anything at
all, you must *see* it before you *receive* it. That is the simplicity of
faith. Matthew 11:22 is explicit—your faith must be in God. Then
Jesus proclaims the spiritual law of faith: Believe you have it before
you get it, or you won't get it! You must see things as you desire
them to be, or you won't receive them.

Several years ago, I was helping my good friend Dr. Charles
Shaffer move into a new home. As I lay under his bed attempting
to attach a long and very heavy solid oak board to the framework,
the weight of the plank shifted, causing it to fall and barely graze
my eyebrow. I hardly even felt it, but the weight of the board was
sufficient enough to cleave my skin and start a flow of blood that
needed to be stopped. Fortunately, Dr. Shaffer's office was a short
distance from his home, and we walked over so that he could close
the wound.

As I lay on the examining table in Chuck's office, I began to
ask him what it was like sewing someone's skin back together.
"How did you learn?" "What does it feel like?" And then I asked a
question whose answer changed the way I approached everything
from then on: "Is it sometimes hard to see what you're doing when
sewing people up like this?"

His answer to this question opened a new horizon of understanding to me. Chuck told me that sewing up a cut like mine
was child's play compared to what doctors do in microsurgery.
Intrigued, I asked him to explain, and he told me that in order to
pass a specific examination in medical school, he had to successfully sew two human hairs together, end to end! What?!

I guess that my jaw dropping to the floor was enough to prompt Chuck to lean over my face, smile, and say matter-of-factly, "Greenman, if you can see it, you can do it."

Ding! Ding! Ding! The bells and whistles went off. I saw it! That is what belief and faith are all about. That is what achievement is all about. If you can see it, you can do it! Amazing!

Now I realize that some of you reading this will be saying, "So what, Greenman? I learned that in second grade in Finger Painting 101." But for me, it was a revelation! It wasn't so much that I didn't already know the principle, because I had been using it for many years by that time. It was the simplistic articulation of it that captured my attention. I'll never forget it. Now you won't, either.

> "If you don't know what the end result looks like,
> you can't get there."
> —*Vince Lombardi*

My First Mind Movie

The first time I experienced this "see it" principle, which is now widely taught in just about every motivational success seminar worth its price, I was a senior at Boca Raton High School in 1971. We had a new coach for our championship track team, and he was just plain fun. We all loved him. Coach Bill Harvey helped me take my pole vaulting to a new and more rewarding level using this technique.

Harv, as we called him, taught me how to "see" myself sprint down the runway; plant the tip of my fiberglass vaulting pole in the wooden box at the base of the foam landing pit; rock back; push with my left hand and pull with my right; pick up my feet and thrust them over the bar as I rotated my hips 180 degrees; push the pole away; and throw my head back to land on my back.

He told me to play that mind movie over and over again in my head before each vault. I had never before heard of doing such a thing, even though I unknowingly had done it before almost every vault, just from nervousness. I just never had been conscious of doing it until Harv explained that I should do so deliberately. I complied. Before every vault, I'd replay that mental movie again and again. As I continued this routine for several weeks, my skills increased and my confidence grew with each new personal best height!

I reached a new skill level that year. When other vaulters struggled with the wind or the sun in their faces, I simply played the mind movie a few more times and vaulted. I don't remember ever having a problem with the elements. They were there, but they just didn't affect me because they were not in my movie! I hit my highest height that year. I found my best form. I won awards. I was not the best, but I hit my personal best! I took that master principle and applied it to everything I did from then on.

"The most interesting people are the people with the most interesting pictures in their minds."
—*Earl Nightingale*

By faith we understand that the worlds were prepared by the word of God, so that what is seen was not made out of things which are visible. (Hebrews 11:3)

Picture What You Want

Would you like to act, speak, or walk in a different way than you presently do? Would you like to be someone of noteworthy style? It begins with a choice you make in the movie studio of your mind. By simply and deliberately imagining the kind of person you wish be, you can become that person. Every child does this. It doesn't require a great education degree; it simply takes a decision to use your imagination on purpose.

> "Imagination is the mother of our creativity."
> —*Bill Greenman*

There are no hindrances in our imagination, no one telling us it can't be done. There are no skeptics or dream stealers. There's only pure belief. We must learn to see exactly what we want—our goals—and then bring those pictures into the reality of our visible realm.

My Son Was a Drug Addict

When my son was thirteen years old, taking acid, shooting heroin, and snorting cocaine, I had to work very hard at seeing him as I *wanted* him to be. I prayed a lot. I'd picture myself standing next to him on a ministry platform sharing the Word of God together and ministering to people. For two years, I fed my spirit God's promises about children from the Word of God. I turned again and again to Deuteronomy 28 to study the curse of the law. I knew that by understanding the curse of the law, I could believe God for the *opposite* of the curse, according to Galatians 3:13–14:

> *Christ redeemed us from the curse of the Law, having become a curse for us—for it is written, "Cursed is everyone who hangs on a tree"—in order that in Christ Jesus the blessing of Abraham might come to the Gentiles, so that we would receive the promise of the Spirit through faith.*

I knew that what Daniel was doing was the opposite of what he was put on the planet to do. He seemed to be slipping away from his destiny and from us. So, I pictured him and my other children always with me until they were grown and on their own. It wasn't easy. Every night, it was a completely different picture in front of me. But I wouldn't give up. Eventually, after seeing what I wanted for Daniel, I needed to apply the second big master principle to achievement: *saying* what I believed.

BIG MASTER PRINCIPLE #2: SAY IT

> *But having the same spirit of faith, according to what is written, "I BELIEVED, THEREFORE I SPOKE," we also believe, therefore also we speak.*   (2 Corinthians 4:13)

This verse is quite simple. It goes hand in hand with Mark 11:22–24, which we just discussed. According to Jesus' teachings on faith, we are required both to believe or to *see* what we want and then to *speak* what we see. Speaking is not just an option for us if we wish to fulfill our God-ordained purpose. Speak specifically what you desire, leaving no question about what you mean.

Gain control of what you believe and what you say, and put them together to unleash the power of God for whatever you seek to achieve. I'm not talking about positive affirmation here. I'm talking about filling your mouth with words wrapped in belief in God! When you get to the point where you can clearly see your dreams and confidently speak them, miracles can take place.

> *For the mouth speaks out of that which fills the heart.*
>   (Matthew 12:34)

> *Death and life are in the power of the tongue, and those who love it will eat its fruit.*   (Proverbs 18:21)

Our words are so powerful that they have the ability to bring us life and death. Our words can set our lives on fire or guide us to safe havens. It's our words, backed by the belief born of constant imagining, visualizing, and seeing, that direct our lives. We will always speak what we believe. We will always believe what we think about the most.

> "When we speak, the hosts of heaven,
> or the hordes of darkness, go to work to bring it to pass."
> —*Bill Greenman*

As I mentioned, my son was a drug addict for over two years. I spent much time deliberately imagining him as God and I wanted him to be, not as he was. As my heart overflowed with visions of him, I began to speak them. I told everyone whom I felt could understand that someday, Daniel would be drug-free, he would be my best friend, and that we would work and minister together.

I told Daniel that, too. He only laughed and said that he didn't believe in God. He said that he was going to be a street person and leave home when he was sixteen. I told him that he would never leave and that I would see him grow up with us. He told me that I was an idiot, and he did run away, but he came back. After, he was arrested and put into juvenile detention with a possible prison sentence. I said that he would not be raised by another, and then found out that he was sentenced only to probation and came home. He ran away while on probation. I said that he would come back and that we would see him grow up with us. He was recaptured. At that point, prison looked imminent again, but I said that he would live only with us. The last time he was before the judge, all charges were dropped, and he came home!

Many miracles took place during the years my son was on drugs. But one day, the greatest miracle of all occurred. He came to me and, with tears in his eyes, told me that he had to give his life to God because he couldn't take it anymore. A few days later at the Brownsville Revival in Pensacola, Florida, I kneeled with him as he made Jesus the Lord and Master of his life! It was glorious.

After, however, I was puzzled that I'd shed no tears on that day. I asked the Lord if there was something wrong with me. His reply was simple and to the point: *You already lived this moment and shed your tears long ago.* I realized that He was right in that I had already played the scenario in my mind so many times and with such conviction that I spoke and believed it as a fact for months. When the event finally had happened, I had already been there and lived it. That is the glory of these master principles of achievement.

"You can and do have what you say."
—*Bill Greenman*

BIG MASTER PRINCIPLE #3: DO IT

"Apply yourself. Get all the education you can, but then, by God, do something. Don't just stand there, make it happen!"
—*Lee Iacocca*

Why do you call Me, "Lord, Lord," and do not do what I say? Everyone who comes to Me and hears My words and acts on them, I will show you whom he is like: he is like a man building a house, who dug deep and laid a foundation on the rock; and when a flood occurred, the torrent burst against that house and could not shake it, because it had been well built.

(Luke 6:46–48)

You see that faith was working with his works, and as a result of the works, faith was perfected...For just as the body without the spirit is dead, so also faith without works is dead.

(James 2:22, 26)

This may sound contradictory, but I want to be sure you don't think that mental pictures and spoken words are *all* you need in order to reach your goals. It ain't so! If you want to enjoy what you see and have what you say, you must do something, as well.

All we've spoken of in previous chapters will do you no good if left on a page. If you're to prove that you can and will accomplish what you believe is your purpose, then you will have get busy to make it happen. You can't get by with lip service and dreams. You have to put muscle into it and act on what you believe. If you say you believe it yet never do it, you never really believed it at all.

If you want to be counted among the achievers, you must go beyond listening and talking and take action. If you don't, your life will be as unstable as the man who built a house on sand. (See Matthew 27:26–27.) Storms will come. Tough times will come. If you haven't acted upon what you believe, you'll have nothing to hold on to.

> *In all labor there is profit, but mere talk leads only to poverty.*   (Proverbs 14:23)

It's our experience that gives us the strength to go on in tough times. I could have watched all the pole-vault mind movies I wanted and talked about how wonderful they were, but if I hadn't picked up my vaulting pole and made the jump, nothing would have happened. Truth is like that. It works when you work it. Then it becomes unstoppable.

> "Some people dream of worthy accomplishments,
> while others stay awake and do them."
> —*Anonymous*

Your purpose is to be performed, not just spoken. If you hang out on the sidelines of your life, you'll be disappointed when the game's over. All the coaching, training, and visualization will be meaningless if you don't go do something. If you don't have a strong work ethic, a desire to work hard at something, then you had best immediately acquire it. Without a desire to perform the very things you discover, there will be little of it to enjoy.

"The opportunity of a lifetime must be seized within the lifetime of the opportunity."
—*Leonard Ravenhill*

Let me share an example. Earlier, I spoke of the slack-wire act I performed. In Florida State University's Flying High Circus, where I learned that act, performers usually walked slowly and carefully to the center of the slack wire and performed different balancing tricks, such as juggling or balancing objects, or even riding a unicycle. It was usually a slow act, with stationary balancing as the primary goal.

However, I was never satisfied with doing what everyone else did. I wanted a new twist. One day, while thinking about that, I had an idea flash into my head: Why not run on the wire? I liked that! No one was doing that or had done that, whom I knew of.

"Bold, overwhelming action is your path to unlimited achievement!"
—*Bill Greenman*

That night during practice at Calloway Gardens Resort in the mountains of western Georgia, the FSU circus' summer home, I set up my rig and began to sing a tune with a very fast beat in my head, while I simultaneously pictured myself running end to end on the wire, again and again. I played this mental movie over and over for several minutes and then got up on the wire to give it a go.

I took two or three quick steps and fell off onto the wooden stage with a smack! (Fortunately, for me, slack wire is performed only about six feet in the air!) I got back up and tried again. Same result. Smack! And again, smack! And again, smack! And again, smack! Smack! Smack! I must have fallen forty or fifty times that night, but I never once felt discouraged because I had a vision of what I wanted to do and the incentive of being the first to do it. My fellow performers and coaches thought I was having an unusually bad practice session.

It took me about a week or so to master running on the wire. It added an excitement to my act that had not previously been there. It kindled a new confidence in me. I also learned another lesson: Be willing to look foolish while going for your goals!

> "Some people wait so long for their ship to come in,
> their pier collapses."
> —*John Goddard*

FINAL THOUGHTS: CONFRONT YOURSELF

Seeing, saying, and then taking action on what you believe often requires confronting yourself. By this I mean that you must be completely honest with yourself about where you are presently. Mind movies and words without action are hollow! You must honestly assess where you are in relation to achieving your purpose. Then you need to act in such a way as to catapult yourself to the next level of accomplishment.

Your biggest struggle will be with inertia. Inertia is the force that holds a rocket on a launch pad after the engine begins to fire. It takes more power to get a rocket moving upward in the first few seconds than it does to project it into orbit! Once it's moving, it takes less and less energy to keep flying. This is true of you, as well.

When you say yes to any one of your goals, you'll experience the power struggle to get off square one and keep moving. Procrastination, discouragement, and many other distractions will try to keep you on the launch pad, so you must expend whatever energy is necessary to keep going forward! Don't let yourself buy the lie that thinking and saying are all it takes—it's action that sets us free from the gravitational pull of lethargy and unbelief. You must *act* on what you believe, or nothing will happen! So, just do it—with a smile!

14

BUT WHAT CAN I DO TODAY?

"Success is never having to say, 'I should have.'"
—*Bill Greenman*

I realize that some of you may have been trying to figure out what your life is all about for many months, years, or even decades. Perhaps you've even applied some or all of the principles we've covered in this book. You've tried it all, yet you still haven't figured out what you're supposed to do with your life. If you're discouraged, it's understandable—but not hopeless!

Don't lose heart. I have good news for you—the Lord does have something for you to do, and you don't have to wait another ten years or even ten days to put it into practice. You can do it now! It's so simple that you may have already thought of it yourself yet shrugged it off as just another shot in the dark. But this is not that; this works! Here it is: If you haven't yet found your personal purpose, then join with someone who has found his. Then do anything and everything you can to help him achieve it. That's right—give yourself to another's vision instead of waiting for lightning to strike for you.

BE ENCOURAGED

God knows that you're seeking Him, and He'll reveal to you His perfect plan for your life. Don't even question that. But it's very likely that the reason you've discovered little of your personal purpose is because He needs your gifts and abilities to help one of His other kids succeed. And that's a great privilege.

Again, this is the universal law of sowing and reaping. We all need each other. Just find someone with a need who can benefit from your gifts, talents, and experience and go to work. No charity has too many volunteers. No person with a vision has too many assistants. Whether it's to a friend's business, a family, or a church, you'll find great fulfillment in giving yourself to others.

> "We must not only give what we have;
> we must also give what we are."
> —*Cardinal Mercier*

When I began our circus ministry, I was also pouring much of my time into the vision of my pastor, and suddenly, something tremendous occurred. I began to receive more plans for *my* vision. It seemed that the more I worked for the church, regardless of what I was doing, the more ideas I'd get about how to start and run my circus. It was the law of sowing and reaping. It was working for me because I was working it. It'll work for you, too! In fact, it's been working your whole life.

Will your plan come to you immediately after you begin to give your time and effort to someone else's purpose? I honestly don't know. However, I do know that you'll be opening yourself up to a return on what you've given. Along with that will come the satisfaction of seeing another's purpose and destiny come to pass before your eyes due to your efforts. Such on-the-job training can prove invaluable when it comes to walking out your own plan.

You'll also be able to learn from the mistakes and successes of the people you work for, and you'll be positively affecting the lives of others at the same time. Furthermore, there's a good possibility that the very people you help will be the same people who help you with your purpose later on. No matter how you slice it, you always come out with good!

So don't get discouraged if you haven't yet discovered your purpose. Instead, be encouraged by the opportunity to learn from others as you prepare. Even if you never receive a full-blown purpose of your own, you will discover that being a part of another person's vision is just as rewarding. In fact, the *majority* of Christians' destinies are wrapped up in the purposes of others. How do I know that? Because as I've said before, no one is an island. No believer is destined to a life of singular accomplishment. We all need the whole body of Christ working together. We need one another. That's the beauty of it all!

HARNESS THE POWER OF PATIENCE

Those of you who do have a vision, a distinct purpose for your life, who may have even received one since starting this book, I have exciting news for you. If you have a purpose but have been struggling to walk it out and feel that you may never see your destiny fulfilled, here is a solid rock upon which to stand:

> For the vision is yet for the appointed time; it hastens toward the goal and it will not fail. Though it tarries, wait for it; for it will certainly come, it will not delay.   (Habakkuk 2:3)

The Lord promises here that every purpose, vision, and destiny has an appointed time and that it will race toward the finish line. It *will* come to pass. It *will* be done. It *will* see fruition. Just hang on! Sure, the wait can be frustrating, wanting to see the plan unfold a bit faster. But don't let discouragement shut you down. Keep going. Stay excited about your goals. Take a look at how far you've come. Get out your destiny plan and daydream about it again. It *is* on the way! Your vision *will* happen!

> *Therefore, do not throw away your confidence, which has a great reward. For you have need of endurance [patience], so that when you have done the will of God, you may receive what was promised....But My righteous one shall live by faith; and if he shrinks back, My soul has no pleasure in him. But we are not of those who shrink back to destruction, but of those who have faith to the preserving of the soul.*
>
> (Hebrews 10:35–36, 38–39)

Did you get that? God told us *not* to throw away our confidence. What confidence is He talking about? Your confidence in Him and in yourself. That's right, *in yourself*! You see, if you throw away your confidence in you, you have nothing to work with. God has confidence in you. He trusts you enough to give you the purpose and destiny that will steer your life. He trusts you enough to give you a vision that will enlist the lives of others. If *He* has that kind of trust and confidence in you, *you* can and must, too!

Don't throw away your confidence in God, either. He has yet to come up against an obstacle in one of His children's lives that's a surprise or is more than He can handle, and you won't be the first! Jesus said, *"With God all things are possible"* (Matthew 19:26). Between you and God, you have everything you need to be a divine success.

Having patience is a challenge for most of us, especially those with a definite purpose to achieve. We so want to accomplish it that we're quite willing to run leagues ahead of anyone and everyone involved. But that's not how a truly confident person acts. The confident person is one who is content to wait for the right timing.

"I do not think that there is any other quality so essential
to success of any kind as the quality of perseverance. It
overcomes almost everything, even nature."
—*John D. Rockefeller*

FIGHT FOR IT

I wish I could say that you'll never face discouragement, but
that would be a lie. Discouragement is a chief weapon of the devil,
but you have far greater weapons and far superior power.

Proverbs 4:20–22 explains that the Word of God is life to
those who find it. Hebrews 4:12 states that God's Word is filled
with power. When discouragement closes in, use God's Word to
push it back into the darkness where it belongs! The Bible is our
sword, and we must be skillful with it.

Here are a few verses I use to encourage myself when my destiny seems to be on hold. Speak them boldly and out loud. Speak
them with *fire* in your heart. If you do, discouragement will run
from you like darkness from the light!

And Jesus said to [the father with the possessed child], "'*If
You can?' All things are possible to him who believes.*"
(Mark 9:23)

*And my God shall supply all your needs according to His
riches in glory in Christ Jesus.*   (Philippians 4:19)

*But thanks be to God, who gives us the victory through our
Lord Jesus Christ.*   (1 Corinthians 15:57)

*But thanks be to God, who always leads us in triumph in
Christ, and manifests through us the sweet aroma of the
knowledge of Him in every place.*   (2 Corinthians 2:14)

But in all these things we overwhelmingly conquer through Him who loved us. (Romans 8:37)

You are from God, little children, and have overcome them; because greater is He who is in you than he who is in the world. (1 John 4:4)

For whatever is born of God overcomes the world; and this is the victory that has overcome the world—our faith. (1 John 5:4)

No weapon that is formed against you shall prosper; and every tongue that accuses you in judgment you will condemn. This is the heritage of the servants of the LORD. (Isaiah 54:17)

FINAL THOUGHTS

With a purpose in your heart and a plan in your hands—even if it belongs to someone else—you're walking in the highest form of living. To know that the plan laid before you is the *perfect* will of the almighty God who created you, and to know that *He* is going to help you and send others to assist you, is the ultimate experience. It brings peace, joy, and life. Nothing compares to walking with God! Go for it with all you've got, and never, ever give up. *You can do it!*

15

SONDANCE – A TESTIMONY

HOW IT'S WORKED FOR THIRTY-PLUS YEARS

In 1980, I had the privilege of meeting two wonderful young ladies, Yvonne Peters and Joanne Cercere, who were starting a new Christian dance ministry called Sondance. When I met these two lovely women, I didn't realize the magnitude of their gifts or the vastness of the call on their lives. Over the next several years, our friendship grew, and we spent many wonderful times together planning their vision. They took the principles discussed in this book and created a powerful "in demand" ministry.

Their progress since our first meeting has taken them around the world many times over, and has inspired hundreds of thousands of believers. This chapter includes the highlights from two interviews I had with them, which are about twenty-five years apart. I believe you'll agree with me that their story is timeless, challenging, and inspiring.

THE FIRST INTERVIEW

B. G. (Bill Greenman): "Why did you come to talk to me that first time?"

Sondance: "We came at that point because we were frustrated in our ministry. We wanted to do everything, but didn't really know how to go about doing anything. From time to time, people would call us to dance at conferences or do local events, but not often. We were dancing only a couple of times a year back then. If we came up with a special piece, we could do it at our home church on Sunday, but we weren't ministering on a regular basis. Our dancing had a purpose to it, and we knew we were called to dance as a ministry, but we didn't know where to go from there."

B. G.: "What happened when you left my office that day?"

Sondance: "We left realizing we needed to state the purpose of our ministry. It caused us to refocus our thinking. We knew we had to think about what we were truly trying to accomplish and how to refine it. We wanted to minister to the church at large. So we decided to organize our priorities and focus on what we felt God was asking of us. We found that many of the things we had a heart to do weren't part of our call."

B. G.: "How did you go about organizing and focusing?"

Sondance: "You spoke that day about planning. But when we came to you that morning, we were not able to plan eighteen *days* ahead. We didn't know what to plan, let alone how to plan. Now, just two years later, we're getting ready to plan an eighteen-*month* calendar!"

B. G.: "As I remember, we talked that day about planning practice sessions and prayer times."

Sondance: "That's right. And that changed our entire course. It gave us a plan to start walking in. We didn't know how to set goals. In our immaturity, we simply expected divine illumination; but after receiving your counsel, the Lord told us, 'Now you have to begin to use what I've given you and pick up the responsibility for what I have ahead of you.' We had projects strewn from one end of the spectrum to the other, but we were too encumbered by work.

By refocusing and setting some goals and priorities, we knew how to accomplish much more than we had in the past."

B. G.: "What did you specifically do in your planning sessions?"

Sondance: "We practiced reverse planning—beginning where we wanted to end up and coming back from there. Then we knew which direction to go first. We also learned not to set ten million goals, but instead to concentrate on two and see if we could accomplish those."

B. G.: "How did that help?"

Sondance: "One of the things you talked to us about was enlisting partners. You told us about intercessors—people who would pray for our ministry. Prior to that time, we had told people, 'We are ministering one week out of the year. Please pray for us as we go.' That had been the extent of our prayer needs. Then God began to deal with our own prayer lives, pushing us to organize a daily prayer time. We focused that time on our goals.

"As we began to pray more specifically, God laid an intercessory foundation in us. He then told us that He would send intercessors to help us pray for our goals. We began to look for them. Out of nowhere, people began to come up and say, 'God has laid you on my heart.' We began to send out intercessor letters, giving people monthly prayer needs and goals. As we laid this foundation of setting practical goals and praying for them, the ministry changed drastically for the better.

"Another major benefit was that we finally focused on what our true ministry was. We had experienced some frustration because we thought that our ministry had to be to the church, to the lost, *and* to support missions. We had tried to reach all those goals but never had been successful. Finally, we realized that our ministry was to the church."

B. G.: "So you had to be careful not to let the dictates and needs of others direct your purpose and define your destiny."

Sondance: "Right. We had the vision, but we placed the wrong criteria on that vision. That changed as we matured."

B. G.: "Why do you think goal-setting and prayers from others were so effective?"

Sondance: "It was the seed principle you mentioned to us. The seed God had given you, you gave to us. That impartation became a new vision in us. What you gave us caused us to focus our vision, which was then able to multiply. Now God will do even more through those who have been seeded by us. When we took the seed of the purpose and destiny God had placed in us, wrote it down, and shared it with others, we gave God the chance to give all recipients their own vision and dream for their lives."

BG: "What are some of the things you've been able to accomplish in the last two years?"

Sondance: "First of all, God began to teach us to move people to worship through our dance, so we began to hold dance workshops in various churches. Those workshops developed into dance troupes, which are now multiplying themselves. The Lord also gave us dance routines involving more dancers than just the two of us. Soon after that came opportunities to choreograph for groups of people and to be a part of worship teams at major conferences.

"Also, God gave us an idea for a workshop which we were invited to share with the dancers who assembled at the Feast of Tabernacles conference in Jerusalem. We're involved with the regional workshops and have worked with hundreds of dancers from churches throughout the southeastern states. We choreographed "The Gospel According to Scrooge," and over fifty thousand people came to see it that year! We also directed the Festival of Praise in Tampa, Florida. That was the largest dance group we had ever worked with—over forty-three dancers, plus children."

B. G.: "That's quite impressive in just two years! Give us some of the positive aspects of discovering your purpose and walking out your destiny while applying all these different principles."

Sondance: "One of the best was that we were able to go full-time in the dance ministry, which was, of course, the dream in our hearts from the beginning. It was the discipline and organization we put into practice that enabled us to be full-time ministers.

"One of the things you said at that first meeting was, 'Can you believe for a salary from the ministry?' At that point, we were supporting the ministry! Your words echoed in our minds, and we talked about it later that week. *Can* we believe? We could! So we began to plan for it, and now the ministry does pay us a salary.

"We also believe one of the most important things you said to us was to get a vision for each goal. After that meeting with you, we listed everything that was happening in our ministry and wrote 'Get a vision' over each item. That caused us to pray and open ourselves up to receive the vision for them. We had to have a different mind-set. That mindset—having a vision for each item, or a picture of what it needs to look like—has changed everything."

B. G.: "What does 'vision' mean to you?"

Sondance: "Vision is created by concentrating on one thing at a time, praying for and meditating on it. In the past two years, many parts of our purpose have found completion. Now God is opening up new areas of our purpose to us.

"Some things we had a vision for did *not* come to pass. That doesn't mean that they have completely died; the timing is just not right yet. However, if we hadn't looked for them, thought about them, and prayed about them in the first place, we probably would have dismissed them completely. It's not that we immediately see things crystal clear. The Lord gives us things to pray about, and that starts the vision process."

B. G.: "Are you saying that God revealed the next step to you as you went along, and not all of them at once?"

Sondance: "Exactly. Also, we've learned to look at it from God's perspective and not our own. It's like looking down and seeing the whole picture rather than our isolated point. Also, I think purpose is different from goals. I think we had mixed them up and were trying to reach our vision in terms of it being a goal. Our vision was much too vast to accomplish as one goal; we had to break it down into several separate goals."

B. G.: "Do you mean that you must have a purpose before you can have a goal?"

Sondance: "That's right. If you don't have the purpose first, you *can't* have a goal. You showed us how to set goals for our purpose. Some things we could work on immediately, so we started there. Others were still in the vision stage, and the only goal we had was to pray for more details on them. At first, we didn't know about short- and long-term goals; we thought everything had to be immediate."

B. G.: "What are the problems you encountered in discovering and living out your purpose in such an organized manner?"

Sondance: "Some of my [Yvonne's] frustrations are that I am not as organized as I would like to be. I would really like to refine things. This kind of organization showed me how unorganized I really am."

"But also, I [Joanne] am an organizer by nature. I start organizing big things and organize down. Suddenly I have organized so much, I have no time for the meat or the creativity. That's a flaw I know I battle."

"We are learning to combat frustration by allocating and are in the process of trying to develop a helps ministry. Two people can't run this ministry anymore; it is much bigger than the two of us. We are so encompassed in the network of organization that we hardly ever have time to create. We are starting to get stale."

B. G.: "You mean you can get so caught up in the business of administrating your vision that you end up planning all the time and leave no time for creativity?"

Sondance: "Yes. Management becomes the goal, and you can't let that happen. The strength of our ministry was that we prayed together, danced together, and worshipped together. Those three things we find very hard to do anymore for lack of time."

B. G.: "Would you say that time management is an important aspect of your purpose?"

Sondance: "Absolutely! And still there is frustration with scheduling. We have to say no to some requests for our ministry. We used to accept anyone who asked us to come. Now we have to go to our calendar and ask, 'Can we?' Time management has definitely been good for us—both daily and long-range."

B. G.: "So two years ago, you had a vision. You knew that God was calling you to a dance ministry, but you didn't know exactly how to go about it. You had come to the place that you were doing everything you knew how to do, but you were not progressing."

Sondance: "We had a call, but I'm not sure we had a vision or purpose. When we came to you, we just knew that what we were doing was God. Up until then, we had been dancing and ministering for five years—not a lot, but it was a valid ministry. In the last two years, however, it has exploded."

B. G.: "So where are you now in your purpose?"

Sondance: "We still have some goals planned for this year that haven't yet been accomplished. That's the nice thing about knowing your purpose and having it planned out. If something doesn't get done today, it will still be there tomorrow. The goals we don't accomplish this year will be first on the list next year."

THE SECOND INTERVIEW

In the 1990s, Yvonne and Joanne ended Sondance and stepped into their individual destinies. They were still the closest of friends and performed with each other at times, but their purposes had taken decidedly different paths. I believe you'll find this interview quite revealing.

After the end of Sondance, Yvonne continued to pursue the ministry of dance in worship, eventually forming Without End Ministries in 1992. Over the ensuing years, she teamed with other internationally recognized dance worship leaders featured in the Feast of Tabernacles festival in Jerusalem, Israel. Yvonne has also ministered in many national and international events, by enlisting the services of dancers from many nations.

Yvonne's average yearly schedule includes four large special events; thirty-five-plus standard church events; fifteen dance/worship workshops; and several large annual events, including the Feast of Tabernacles in Israel; several Feast of Tabernacle events across the U.S.; Passovers; and Hanuakkah events. Yvonne travels over one hundred thousand air miles per year, having ministered in ten nations—most frequently in Russia and Israel.

YVONNE'S EXPERIENCE

B. G.: "Yvonne, has your purpose or destiny changed at all since you and Joanne ended Sondance?"

Yvonne: "My destiny has changed and continues to change step-by-step through my maturing process, but my purpose remains the same. Some parts of my earlier vision were *me*-oriented, which have changed to be more *Christ*-oriented. God warned me not to let pride and flattery get strongholds in my life. That powerfully affected me, and I have not forgotten it.

"Numbers are irrelevant when it comes to ministering to people—ten or ten thousand people should be the same. I remember you told me, 'Yvonne, you are a pioneer, and pioneers never stop being pioneers—they keep breaking new ground.' That's true. I am never satisfied to stay where I am *now*. I want to press into another realm in worship with dance. I want a greater release of God's presence and what His presence will do for people. I want to go cross-cultural and cross-denominational. That takes pioneering."

B. G.: "What other areas have you been growing in?"

Yvonne: "Mentoring. The 'live your life with' folks are different than those you minister to. People you know have the same burning passion you have and are willing to give it all...those are the type of people I want to share my skills and experience with and whom I've been looking for. I am getting more and more bookings. I'm doing more teachings, spending more time in each location. You told me that I would spend more time like this—taking more time to impart in others rather than just hit-and-run. You also told me to reproduce myself in video and audio teachings, and I have several available now. Sowing the seeds of your life into others should be a key in every person's destiny."

B. G.: "What about finances—how have you fared in that realm?"

Yvonne: "There has never been volumes of cash in our ministry, but since 1985, when I went full-time, there has always been provision for all God told me to do. I have no big bank accounts, but all has been supplied, and I've traveled the world in comfort. To do all the Lord has for me to do—that is success. But I am daily praying for wisdom in this area."

B. G.: "What are some of the personal parts of your destiny in which you've seen changes?"

Yvonne: "I'm a grandmother now. My daughter has danced with me several times, with a local troupe of worship dancers. I've learned a lot about dealing with a troupe long-term, and it's been wonderful. It's given me a venue to try new ideas and teachings and so forth. My friends have been able to bring to light my weaknesses and improve my ministry and life. You can't get that from people you meet on the road. You must have such a group if you are doing what I do.

"I have mentors who have experience with ministry, and I run all spiritual things by them. I believe artists need this kind of critical input. Your art is so tied up in you that you must have people keeping you honest. I also have a board, which has been instrumental in helping me grow and learn and be. They are a working board; they know me and are honest with me."

B. G.: "How do you continue to hold so much activity of life together?"

Yvonne: "Planning! The annual events I plan way ahead, and I have such relationships with all involved. This makes the planning easier. I wait to see what invitations come. There are times that emphasize teaching or demonstrating or training in ministry, and the invitations line that up. Then I plan accordingly."

B. G.: "What would you tell the person who wants to find his purpose in life?"

Yvonne: "In 1980, I asked the Lord for my purpose. A plane flew over at that moment, and the Lord spoke to me, saying, 'You will go to the nations.' I was blown away. At the time, lived in a one bedroom apartment making $120 a week and had no idea what I would do if I did go to some other nation.

"Two decades later, I have been around the world many times. I have learned to believe and to trust and to be obedient at each step. I was faithful in the little things, like going to nursing homes and doing whatever I could put my hand to, before I ever went to the first nation. Don't despise small beginnings, but *never* let go of the first vision! Avoid the traps of ego and pride and wanting fame.

"Your purpose and goals all will be tested. We may be on a shelf in the back for a long period until the right time. Your heart must be in a willing place. My vision did not happen as I thought, and I had to remind and encourage myself during the waiting time. Waiting may mean that God wants you to help build another's vision during that time.

"I worked five years in a doctor's office while my vision burned in my heart. As an artist, that job was uncreative and dry for me, but I learned so many principles of focus and discipline. I needed it. It was invaluable experience. I learned to flow with so many cross-cultural and cross-denominational leaders. If I had not learned that on the shelf, I could not have done it in frontline ministry."

JOANNE'S EXPERIENCE

When Sondance disbanded, Joanne became a third-grade teacher in a local Christian school. She held both adult and children's dance classes. She also helped direct dance groups in her home church. During the summer months when school was not in session, Joanne traveled, holding dance workshops and ministering in local fellowships. She also worked with several area churches on special events and occasionally ministered in conferences around the U.S. and other nations.

B. G.: "Joanne, give us an idea of the transition you experienced after Sondance."

Joanne: "My last dance with Yvonne in Sondance was at the 1990 Feast of Tabernacles in Israel. I came back financially broke, because even though the ministry was doing well, our financial needs were rising. I sought counsel and decided that a job was a must. By January, I was teaching first grade; but at the end of the school year, the school permanently closed after twenty years of service! So I thought I'd be back in full-time ministry after that, but that wasn't God's plan. I took a job the next fall at another school, and I've never left the classroom since.

"After years of traveling around the world, culture shock set in! But being a teacher allows me to use the summers for ministry at dance, drama, and mime camps. I also minister in worship conferences each summer, sometimes overseas. So, to a small extent, I've kept my hand in performing ministry.

"Every year, I felt that teaching would end and dance would begin again. Now I know that dance will never again be what it was for me, even though I'll probably be doing something in the arts and teaching.

"Now my burden, my destiny, has shifted, though my purpose of ministering to people remains the same. Whereas before I was ministering and training others in worship through dance, now I see a three-phase destiny.

"Phase one of my destiny involves working with *children* of the next generation and those after them, who have taken my heart. They are my children, as I don't have my own. I'll work with them in dance or teaching or whatever God asks of me.

"Phase two involves *healing* the people [not nations] of the earth. I do inner-city work with African Americans and others using God as the common denominator. I see others' dances as a way to create bridges. I create multicultural dance, bringing people together in dance groups.

"Phase three involves *Israel.* I asked myself, "What can I do beyond dancing at feasts, both in Israel and in the U.S.?" My answer was to share the love of God. That takes relationships. It's always about people, isn't it? So, I'm seeking to build those relational bridges."

B. G.: "Is there one particular life area you've gained specific wisdom in since being on your own again?"

Joanne: "Yes. It's connected to something you told us in our very first meeting back in 1980. You shared with us that a workman is worthy of his hire. In those early ministry years, we had no price list for our ministry, giving guidance as to what to charge when we performed at someone's church or event. We found that if we didn't price our services, we'd received less, and if we did, we usually received more. So we started pricing our services in ministry. But we based price on our *need*, not on our *worth*. It was unbalanced and uncomfortable. We took a lot of bookings for money, and I'm not sure it was always the right thing to do! The line between business and ministry was blurred.

"I wanted to go without needing the money. So now, being independently financed through my job, I'm now secure when I go to minister, as I have no need of money. It is so freeing."

B. G.: "What advice would you give to a person who is searching for his purpose?"

Joanne: "Keep learning through listening and reading. Use good quality methods of confirming everything you desire and seek to achieve, and remember to be a faithful giver. Sowing and reaping is what makes *everything* work."

FINAL THOUGHTS

Joanne Cercere and Yvonne Peters are people just like you and me; they have purposes for their lives just as we all do. But their purposes seemed to take off overnight, and even through a variety of changes, they have continued to shine. Why? Because they *chose* to discover their purposes, both as individuals and as a team, and then live them out. They said yes to the invitation. They embraced their individual calls and ran hard after their destinies. They put action to their faith and saw results on a daily basis.

Joanne and Yvonne achieved their goals and dreams and much more. *You* can do the same, regardless of whether your purpose is to lead thousands of people into intimate worship on a worldwide scale or to be a humble teacher pouring knowledge into the fertile minds of children in a neighborhood school. We all have a call, a place where we will flourish.

I hope these candid reflections on how my two dear friends learned and applied the principles of purpose and destiny will inspire you to do the same with your life.

If you have more questions or want to learn more, be sure to look at our resources in the next few pages or on our Web site. I couldn't possibly put everything from a lifetime of research and experience into one book, and I'm sure some of our other resources could help you on your own journey of unlocking your purpose and living your destiny.

RESOURCES

One of my lifetime goals has been seeking out coaches and mentors to help learn and grow in the areas I seek to improve and fulfill my own purpose. This has led me to create several coaching products, which include audio, video, print, and private one-on-one sessions. Be sure to visit my Web site, www.purpose3.com, to discover how my coaching expertise can help you acquire the principles you need to live your life to the fullest. Visit www.Purpose3.com to browse my blogs, books, audios, videos, e-courses, and so forth, for all things dealing with personal purpose and destiny, covenant realities, relationships, and more.

You can also follow me on, Facebook, Twitter, and LinkedIn.

Send all correspondence to

Bill@Purpose3.com

THE PURPOSE 3 AFFILIATE PROGRAM

Furthermore, I'm all about multiplying my efforts to fulfill my purpose of taking this message of purpose and destiny to the world, but I can't do it alone and don't want to try. So I created this the Purpose 3 Affiliate Program to help others join hands with me and my team. The premise is very simple—whenever you help us sell something through the Web or otherwise, you will receive part of the profit. You can even help enroll others in our affiliate program and earn from what they sell. You don't have to spend any money, stock product, ship product, or even try to talk anyone into anything. All you have to do is use some of our online tools to get your friends to take a look at what we do. That's it. You can find all the details about this program on our Web site under the "Affiliates" tab.

ABOUT THE AUTHOR

Bill Bill Greenman graduated from Florida State University in 1976 and entered into the professional circus world with his wife, Meg. After a disappointing initial season and a disastrous auto accident, the Greenmans ended their short professional circus careers to seek the Lord's will for their lives. One year later they combined their professional circus skills with their desire to win souls for Christ and began Circus Alleluia Ministries (CAM).

Over the ensuing eleven years Bill directed CAM's many outreaches, training more than sixty volunteers in circus and ministry, while taking the circus into prisons, juvenile centers, public and private schools, civic auditoriums, and Christian festivals across the eastern half of the US and Canada, including a feature on CBN's *The 700 Club*. That decade of ministry saw tens of thousands of people won to Christ.

In 1980, after his own miraculous healing from double pneumonia, Bill began to experience dramatic manifestations of the Holy Spirit after Circus Alleluia performances. Thousands of miracles took place when he and members of his troupe prayed for people to be healed and delivered from Satan's hold, some of whom led hundreds more to Christ after sharing their miraculous testimonies. In late 1988 the Lord led the Greenmans to end Circus Alleluia Ministries after fulfilling their final ministry dates.

In spring 1989 Bill and Meg were introduced to Mike Bickle and the brethren at Metro Christian Fellowship in Kansas City, Missouri, and he was asked to join MCF's staff as an associate pastor. He functioned primarily as a counselor during the next two and a half years, with an emphasis on personal deliverance ministry.

In summer 1992 the Greenmans and the leaders of MCF felt the Lord directing Bill to enter the corporate business world. Over the next year Bill helped a friend with the formation of a manu-facturing/retail company that boasted two million dollars in sales within the next eighteen months. In 1994 Bill became involved with a nutraceutical company, and began leading recruiting/train-ing meetings across the US. That same year the Greenmans moved to Dallas, Texas, and Bill became director of promotions for that same company.

In 1997 the Greenmans began Purpose International, a min-istry that directs the planning and production of the many educa-tional tools focused on the finding and fulfilling of God's purpose for the individual Christian. Bill's time is now divided between building his secular businesses and Purpose International on sev-eral continents.

In 2000 Bill was given an honorary Doctorate of Divinity by Life Christian University in Tampa, Florida, where he also earned his Masters in Pastoral Ministry. In 2001 Bill earned his Ph.D. in Practical Theology, also from Life Christian University, and pub-lished his purpose-discovery materials for youth, entitled *Destinies on Edge*. In 2008 Bill completed a 24-week high school-level cur-riculum entitled *How to Find Your Purpose in Life*.

In 2007 Purpose International Ministries–Kenya, Africa, was formed as a CBO to take the purpose message to that conti-nent. Since then, PIMK has been asked to work closely with the Kenyan government's justice department to take this life-changing message to the youth of that nation. This is being done through TV, radio, live youth rallies, church events, and seminars in high schools and college campuses—partially funded by the Kenyan government.

Bill and Meg have lived in the Nashville, Tennessee, area since 2001. They have three grown children and three grandchildren.